GUARD

THE

TREASURE

How God's People
Preserve God's Word

GUARDING THE TREASURE

How God's People Preserve God's Word

Linda Finlayson

CF4·K

10 9 8 7 6 5 4 3 2 1
© Copyright 2011 Linda Finlayson
ISBN: 978-1-84550-683-4

Published by
Christian Focus Publications,
Geanies House, Fearn, Tain, Ross-shire,
IV20 1TW, Scotland, Great Britain.
www.christianfocus.com
email: info@christianfocus.com

Cover design by Daniel van Straaten
Cover illustration by Brent Donoho
Inside Illustrations by Brent Donoho
Printed and bound by Nørhaven, Denmark

*Front cover: William Tyndale gathering together his books and
manuscripts as he flees from his enemies.*
*Back cover: Jo Shetlar Missionary and Translator of the Balangao New Testament
standing beside a child as she holds one of the first New Testaments in the
Balangao language.*

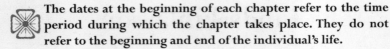 **The dates at the beginning of each chapter refer to the time
period during which the chapter takes place. They do not
refer to the beginning and end of the individual's life.**

* Check the Glossary for unfamiliar words.

For Sandy

Contents

Boxes from the Sky
July 24, 1982

Jo Shetler brushed aside her dark hair and shaded her eyes against the strong sun as she looked up into the clear sky. The planes had been arriving all day in this remote valley in the Philippines, bringing visitors and food for the celebrations. She spied another small plane as it crested the tops of the mountains and circled to land on the airstrip the Balangao people had built years before. She waved her arms excitedly. Maybe this plane had the boxes.

'Juami!'

Jo turned when she heard her Balangao name and saw Tekla, dressed in a colourful striped skirt and white blouse, coming toward her. Tekla had become a dear friend over the years that Jo had lived in this tropical valley among Tekla's people.

'How many more are coming?' Tekla asked as the plane began its descent.

'There'll be eighty Americans at least,' Jo replied with a smile. 'And who knows how many hundreds of Balangaos from all the villages.'

Tekla's brown face lit up with laughter. 'It will be a wonderful party.' Then she turned aside to direct some lost American visitors to the home they would be staying in.

All around them stood wooden houses on four foot stilts, each with a bamboo ladder reaching from the ground to the front door. Thatched roofs topped the bamboo houses and pens full of chickens and pigs occupied the spaces underneath. The village itself was set in the bottom of the deep valley surrounded by terraced rice fields carved out of the mountain sides.

The small plane came to a stop, and Jo went out toward it. The pilot jumped out, waved at her, and then opened the side doors to let his passengers out.

'Good flight, Bob?' Jo asked as she came up behind him.

'Yep,' he replied, assisting an older gentleman down the few steps. 'And,' he added, 'I brought the boxes!'

'May I see them? Now?' Jo asked impatiently

'Only if you promise not to open them until the dedication begins,' Bob teased.

He climbed into the back of the plane and handed out several medium sized wooden boxes one at a time to Jo, who carefully set them down on the ground. Both pilot and missionary stood and looked at the ordinary crates, thinking of the extraordinary things they carried inside of them.

'Congratulations, Jo. This has been a long time coming and you must be very pleased,' Bob said softly.

Jo just nodded, suddenly feeling a surge of tears rising up in her eyes. After a moment she managed, 'Let's take them to my house until it's time. Oh, I can't wait to see Ama's face when he sees them.' Then to hide the tears she bent down to pick up a crate and led the way for Bob and a few recruits to follow her to her house on stilts.

As the procession wound itself through the crowds of people, one figure came sprinting up to them from the far side of the village. He stopped in front of Jo, breathing hard.

'Is this them?' Doming asked.

Jo smiled down at her twenty-year-old adopted brother. Like many of his people, he was only five feet tall. Jo handed him her box. He held it with care, his eyes shining.

'But you can't open it yet,' she said. 'Not till the ceremony. And not until Ama sees them first.'

Doming nodded and gave her a look of understanding. Ama was Doming's father and Jo's adopted father. By rights he should see the contents first.

It was late afternoon when everyone had finally arrived. All the baggage the Americans had brought was stowed in their hosts' houses. The canopies of quilts and palm branches had been set up to shade the seats cut out of the hillside. The aroma of cooking pork filled the air, promising a wonderful feast after the dedication ceremony.

Jo stood looking out over the hundreds of faces, white and brown, as they settled themselves on the seats under the canopies. She listened to their excited chatter in both Balangao and English, and waved or nodded as many looked her way. How she loved the people that God had allowed her to serve for the past twenty years. People like Tekla who had refused to sacrifice to the spirits long before she had heard about Jesus, knowing that she needed to worship the true God. Or little old Forsan, the spirit medium, who, until her conversion, everyone used to call when they needed to appease the evil spirits. Or Andrea, who had been amazed that Jesus could command the evil spirits to leave and they would go. If Jesus was powerful enough to free her, then he was the one she wanted to follow. And dear Ama, Jo's adopted father. Jo gave him a special smile as he made his way toward her through the crowds. Ama had taken her under his wing when she first arrived. He told her she needed someone to look after her since she was a woman and his people were head hunters. Jo was sure he was wrong, but quickly realised he was right. People wouldn't listen to her, but they would listen to her 'father.' He told her the customs of his people, helped her with the language and even insisted she join his family, her family, for dinner each day. Ama didn't understand the gospel though, and it took many years before he was convinced it was safe to reject the spirit worship of his people to serve God. Now he was an evangelist to the other villages in the area.

Ama stood beside Jo, coming up to just past her shoulder. Dressed in a short sleeved white shirt and dark trousers, Ama held up his arms to quiet the crowd. As the chatter slowly ceased a number of other Balangoa grouped themselves around Jo and Ama. These were all the people who had helped Jo with the translation work. Ama had a programme organised and he stepped up to the microphone to begin.

Custom demanded that all visitors must be introduced, and their host families too. Then, after a number of speeches and songs, it finally came time to open the boxes piled nearby. Jo opened the first one, reached in and pulled out a black bound book. Everyone grew silent, so that the only sounds were the humid winds rustling the palm branches and the songbirds of the forests calling and chiming their music. Turning to Ama, she held it out to him, the first copy of the New Testament in his own language. Jo couldn't stop grinning as Ama took it carefully with both hands and held up for all to see.

'This is what we've been waiting for!' he called out, tears leaking out of his eyes. 'And now we will celebrate! Balangao style!'

The crowd erupted into cheering and clapping, and some starting to sing and play gongs. Laughing and crying, Jo reached into the box again and gave out a book to each one who had helped with the translation work over the years. Each accepted his or her copy with care, opening the pages and reading with wonder the stories of Jesus in their own language.

That was just the beginning of a celebration that lasted for two days. Each village that came to the celebration had prepared its own special presentation. Some had written songs to commemorate the coming of God's Word to their valley, others told stories about how they had come to believe and the struggles they had against the spirit world. Jo listened in wonder to those stories. These people had more struggles than she had realised and she praised God for his saving grace and strength among the Balangao people.

* * *

Have you ever thrown a party when you received a Bible as a gift or gone to purchase one at the store? Probably not. While we value God's Word very much, we have so many Bibles all around us that we don't get as excited as the Balangao people did. They were seeing their Bibles for the first time. We, on the other hand, can buy Bibles at any bookstore. We can choose ones with different coloured covers; decide if we want one with pictures or notes, or neither. We can buy inexpensive soft cover ones or very expensive leather ones. Many different versions are available, all in English. The King James Version uses older English words and phrases, like reading a Shakespeare play. There are modern versions, like the New International Version, that read more like the books we get from the library. We can also download the Bible onto our mobile phones or iPad. With so many choices why would we get excited just to get a new Bible?

We are very blessed indeed in our country to have God's Word so easily available to us. But it hasn't always been that way, nor is the Bible available in every place in the world. Like the Balangao people in the Philippines, people long ago did not have many copies of God's Word, or even copies of it in their own language. What Jo Shetler did for the Balangao people, many people in history have done for us. Let's find out who they were and how we got our Bible.

Meet the Writers

The Bible is not actually one book. Rather, it is like a library, a collection of sixty-six books all put together. God inspired many people to write these books at different times in history and then the early church councils put them all together. What sort of people did God ask to write down his message for his people? A slave turned prince, military commanders, an exiled politician, Jewish kings, priests, prophets, a farmer, a fisherman, a doctor, a scholar turned missionary, a former tax collector, and Jesus' own half-brother. These people wrote what God inspired them to write. And they used the gifts that God gave them to write in different styles. Some wrote about the historical events of Israel. Some wrote in poetry and verse. Some wrote biographies of people who loved God. Some told of visions, both wonderful and terrible, that God had given them. Some wrote about how Jesus, God's son, came to earth, lived and died for us and came back to life again! Some wrote letters, giving God's instructions and encouragement to believers.

Let's meet a few of these people and see how God used them in writing his Word ...

Moses
(Around the thirteenth century B.C.[1])

Moses was born a Jewish slave in Egypt at a very dangerous time. Pharaoh, fearful that his slave population was growing too large, had decreed that all baby boys were to be thrown into the River Nile. Moses' parents disobeyed that command and kept him hidden for three months. But, as with all babies, it was difficult to keep the little one quiet. So eventually his parents did obey Pharaoh's decree, but not exactly as Pharaoh meant. Moses' mother made a waterproof basket and placed him inside and set the little boat floating on the river. She chose the right place to do it; just where Pharaoh's daughter came to bathe each morning. When the princess saw little Moses she knew immediately that he was the child of Jewish slaves, but her heart was soft and she decided to adopt him to protect him from death. And so it was that Moses went from being a slave to becoming a prince.

Years later when Moses was grown and living in the palace, he decided to go and see what was happening to his people, the Jewish slaves. He found that they were badly mistreated by cruel overseers. In anger, Moses killed one of the overseers who was beating a slave. Then he hid the body in the sand dunes. But others had seen the crime and reported it to Pharaoh, who became angry with Moses. So Moses ran away, as far as he could go, to the land of Midian. There he became a shepherd, quietly minding his sheep away from all the difficulties in Egypt. But God had a job for Moses to do and called to him from a burning bush. God wanted Moses to go back to Egypt and lead the Jewish people out of that place and into a new

---

[1] B.C. means **B**efore **C**hrist was born.

country. Reluctantly, Moses obeyed. It was not an easy task. Pharaoh saw no reason to let his slave population go. At least not until God sent ten nasty plagues on the land. After the Egyptians had suffered a great deal, Pharaoh finally let Moses lead the Jewish people out.

But Moses' job was not finished. God told Moses to meet him on Mount Sinai, where God gave Moses the Ten Commandments and the rest of the laws he wanted his people to obey. The laws included how God should be worshipped and how the people must behave toward each other. For this reason, Moses has been known as the Law Giver by Jewish people right up until today. How easy Moses' life would have been after that if only God's people had just obeyed what God had commanded. But like all of us, they would forget, or choose to forget, and do what they felt like instead of obeying God. As a result, the people were not allowed to go directly to the Promised Land. Instead, they spent forty years living in the wilderness with Moses as their leader. When at last the people were allowed to go to Canaan, God told Moses that he was only allowed to see the Promised Land from a mountain top before he died.

God had Moses write down the history of the Jewish people from the beginning of Creation to the time just before they entered Canaan. These are the first five books of the Old Testament: Genesis, Exodus, Leviticus, Numbers, and Deuteronomy. These books were originally written down on scrolls. Copies were made through the years and kept in the temple and synagogues to be read out to the people when they came to worship God. These books are called the Torah.

David
(Around 1000 B.C.[2])

David was born into a family of boys in the town of Bethlehem, the youngest of Jesse's eight sons. Jesse owned a great many sheep and David was given the job of looking after them. David enjoyed being out in the pastureland where, as the sheep grazed peacefully, he could play his lyre and compose songs. But it wasn't always peaceful. He had to keep a close eye on the flock, who, not being very bright, could wander off and be injured or eaten by bears or lions. In fact, David had to kill those wild animals when they came too close to the sheep. He was practiced with a sling shot and could aim accurately enough to hit an animal in just the right spot to kill it.

David's life began to change when the prophet Samuel came to Bethlehem and told him and his family that God had chosen David to be Israel's next king. At first it appeared that the message made no difference whatsoever. David went back to taking care of sheep, practising his fighting skills with the sling and shepherd's staff, and composing poems and songs about God and his creation. But shortly after that David ended up facing and defeating the giant Philistine, Goliath. David was then welcomed into King Saul's palace, became a close friend of Jonathan, Saul's son, and married Michal, Saul's daughter. But Saul was jealous of David because God had chosen David to be the next king, and because the Israelites loved David. So Saul tried to kill David.

David went into hiding, but he was not alone. Over time many young men came to join his army, but they didn't fight against Saul. David knew it was wrong to kill someone God had anointed. Only in God's time would David become king. Until then they had to

---

[2] B.C. dates go backward from the birth of Jesus Christ (the opposite of how we count today, because we are counting forward from his birth).

wait patiently. During that time David had a chance to meet many of the people he would one day rule over. David became king when Saul and all his sons were killed in a battle with the Philistines.

David ruled over Israel for forty years. He had many difficulties to deal with: invading armies, rebels in his own army, and problems with his own sons. But he eventually established a peaceful kingdom. God called David 'a man after my own heart.' That meant that David loved God and tried to live as God had commanded. But even David had his failings and there were times when God had to punish David for sinning. And even though he was a king, David was humble and asked God to forgive him. Out of all of this, came the poems or Psalms that David wrote. The Psalms cover all the things that happen in life: praising God for his mighty works, asking God for help during troubled times, confessing sin and asking forgiveness, rejoicing in God's goodness and care. David experienced all these things and used his gift of song-writing to worship God. These Psalms were included in the Old Testament books, used in worship in the synagogues and the temple and have had a central place in the worship of the church.

Jeremiah
(Around 626-585 B.C.)

Jeremiah was born in the town of Anathoth, not far from Jerusalem. His father, Hilkiah, was a priest. King Josiah was ruling in Judah at that time, and wanted to serve God. He had issued orders to repair the temple that had been neglected, and told the people to turn away from idol worship. But the people were stubborn and some refused to turn back to God and worship him. So when Jeremiah was just a young man, God called him to be a prophet, someone who would deliver God's message to the people. God had plenty to say to those stubborn people.

Jeremiah's life was not an easy one. The messages God gave him to preach were not pleasant. Jeremiah was to tell the people that God was angry with them, so angry that he was going to allow an invasion and eventually the people would be captured and taken away to foreign lands. But, God also said that he loved them, and later he would allow them to return and rebuild their land. You can imagine that Jeremiah was not very popular with the people or the kings who came after Josiah. Jeremiah's life was threatened more than once. He suffered beatings, was thrown down a well and put in prison. All of this happened because he faithfully gave God's message. Not only that, but other men, calling themselves prophets too, preached false messages to the people. They said Jeremiah was lying and they were speaking God's truth. There were times that Jeremiah felt very discouraged, but he didn't give up. He did as God told him to, and wrote down the messages in the book named after him in the Bible.

Jeremiah is just one of the many prophets God called to preach warnings and messages of love to his people. Seventeen books in the Old Testament are books written by God's prophets. These books were not just for the Israelites back then, but are meant to be read by Jews and Christians as messages from God that we need to hear today.

Luke
(Around A.D.[3] 60)

Luke was a Gentile, born somewhere outside of Israel. There are no exact dates, but he must have been born sometime around the same time that Jesus was born. Although we know little of Luke's background, we do know that he was well educated. He

---

[3] A.D. refers to the time after Christ's birth. The letters A.D. are a short form for the Latin words Anno Domini, which mean 'Year of our Lord.'

was trained to be a doctor, and was also a writer and historian. At some point in his adult life he became a Christian and met the Apostle Paul. They became good friends and Luke accompanied Paul on his missionary journeys around the Roman Empire. Luke even went with Paul to Rome when Paul was arrested and tried by the emperor. Luke endured much of what Paul did: persecutions and beatings by those who didn't want to hear the gospel, joy when some were converted and new churches begun, tiredness, hunger, shipwrecks and even prison.

Luke wrote two books in the New Testament: the Gospel of Luke and the Acts of the Apostles. The gospel is the story of Jesus' ministry, death and resurrection, and then Luke continues the story of the early Christians and Paul's missionary journeys in Acts. It was like writing books one and two in a series for the early Christians to read and learn about Jesus and the early church. He wrote in what we call a narrative or story telling fashion. Luke said that he wanted to 'write an orderly account'[4] because he knew these events were important and true. And indeed they are. God inspired Luke to record all these events so that we would have a clear historical account of what happened during Jesus' time on earth and the beginning of the early church.

Paul
(Around A.D. 60)

Paul was born around the time of Christ in the city of Tarsus. He was Jewish, but his family also had Roman citizenship. Paul was a bright young man and he did so well at the synagogue school that his family sent him to Jerusalem to be trained as a scholar with Gamaliel, a respected member of the Sanhedrin.

---

[4] See Luke 1:1-4

Paul was a committed follower of God. He wanted to live a life that pleased God and was distressed when others refused to obey God's law. Paul, along with many of the Jewish leaders, didn't believe that Jesus was the Messiah, or that he had come back from the dead. So when the early church began after Jesus' death and resurrection, Paul was concerned that Christians were not following God. He thought they were out to change God's law as laid down in

the Scriptures (what we now call the Old Testament). So he received permission from the Jewish leaders to arrest the Christians and put them in prison. But Jesus himself intervened. He appeared to Paul in a vision and told Paul to stop persecuting Christians and become one of them. Jesus changed Paul's heart so that he understood that Jesus really is the Son of God. Paul became the first Christian missionary. He travelled to as many parts of the Roman Empire as he could, preaching the gospel and establishing churches. Paul endured a lot of hardship, even while he had the joy of seeing so many come to Christ. He experienced beatings, stoning, riots and prison. But he never gave up, telling people that 'I count everything as loss because of the surpassing worth of knowing Christ Jesus my Lord.'[5]

Paul wrote letters to the churches and some individuals, teaching them about God and telling them how they should live to please God. He warned them against false teachers and encouraged them to remember their ultimate goal was to become more like Christ. The early Christians gathered Paul's letters together so that they could be read whenever Christians met for worship. Eventually they became part of the New Testament.

These are five of the many writers of the books of the Bible. God used many more people, inspiring them with messages he wanted his people to hear. Together all these books make up the Bible we have today. But how did all these books, written by so many different writers over a long period of time get together in the one book we now call our Bible?

---

[5] Philippians 3:8a.

How to Make a Book in Ancient Times:

The first 'books' were written on surfaces that people had to hand: flat stone, large wooden tablets and tablets made of clay.

To write on those surfaces people used a variety of tools. Stone tablets required a chisel and hammer and a very precise effort to chip out the letters one by one. You think you have something to complain about when you're asked to write neatly on paper, just imagine if you had to chisel your work out instead.

Wooden tablets were a little more user friendly. In ancient Egypt the scribe's tools included fine brushes, pens and ink which he carried around in a wooden box. Black ink was made from charcoal or soot, but he could also make a variety of coloured inks by crushing minerals and mixing them with water to produce red, green and blue. The brushes and pens were made from papyrus reeds, which wore out quickly so he needed a large supply.

Clay tablets were the most popular of the three. They were easily made from the clay soil, a common and inexpensive item. While the clay was still soft, the writer would use a stylus, made of wood or bone, to jab the clay repeatedly to form the outline of the letters. A bit slow, you might think, but he had to be fairly quick especially if he lived in the hot climates of the Near East because the clay did dry out. When the writing was complete, the clay tablet was then baked to harden it, making it a long lasting 'book.'

Not surprisingly all these items were large, heavy and not easily stored. You would have difficulty lugging around a large stone, which had to be a decent size to have anything of substance written on it. So this medium was generally used for official signs and announcements, something that was put in a public place for all to see. The wooden tablets were sometimes stored in what we call book form today: several tablets on top of one another and bound together by threading pieces of leather through holes in each wooden piece. But the form did restrict the size. Again, wooden tablets were hardly pocket-sized and difficult to read in bed. Clay tablets were long-lasting, but had the same drawback as the stone: large and heavy. Official documents recorded on clay were usually stored on shelves or in labelled wooden boxes, making them easier for the official or librarian to find in large collections.

What is a Canon?

When you hear or read the word *canon*, the first thing you might think of is a large metal weapon used to shoot cannon balls at the enemy from a castle wall or a ship. But that is not the type of canon we mean when we speak of the Canon of the Bible. This word has a very different meaning. Finding out where a word has come from helps us to understand what it means today.

The word 'canon' comes from the Greek word *kanon* that means 'reed' or 'cane' or 'rule' or 'measure.' There is also a similar word in Hebrew *keneh* that means a 'standard of measurement.' From these words comes our English word 'canon,' which means a standard list or set of rules. When we use the word in describing the Bible, we mean that the Bible contains the canon or authorised list of books of the Bible.

But who got to decide what the Canon of the Bible would contain? God, of course. He had planned all along who the writers should be, what they should write and how the entire Bible would be put together. And he used ordinary people to do it.

The Old Testament

The Old Testament books were written first in the Hebrew language over many centuries. As they were gathered together the books were put into categories: the Law or Torah, Historical books, Poetic or Wisdom Literature and the Prophets. The Law or Torah are the first five books written by Moses: Genesis, Exodus, Leviticus, Numbers and Deuteronomy. Next are twelve historical books: Joshua, Judges, Ruth, 1 and 2 Samuel 1 and 2 Kings, 1 & 2 Chronicles, Ezra, Nehemiah and Esther. They tell the history of Israel. Job, Psalms, Proverbs, Ecclesiastes and the Song of Solomon are the wisdom literature or poetic books. And all the prophets' writings (Isaiah, Jeremiah, Lamentations, Ezekiel, Daniel, Hosea, Joel, Amos, Obadiah, Jonah, Micah, Nahum, Habakkuk, Zephaniah, Haggai, Zechariah and Malachi) are gathered at the end. Put these all together and you have thirty-nine books.

They were written on large papyrus scrolls. The Jewish priests took care to preserve these by storing them in the temple and synagogues in special places. The scrolls themselves were wrapped carefully in cloth. Each time the people gathered to worship God, the priests would take out the scrolls, unroll them and read from them. There are many places in the Bible where we are told that when God's Word was read out to the people that they repented of their sin and asked God to help them to obey his commands.

Sometime after the last of the books was written, about 400 years before Jesus was born, the books were all gathered together and called the Canon. This is what we call the Old Testament today. These were the Scriptures that were read in the temple and synagogues on the Sabbath. Jesus himself read and quoted from these books. Luke 4:16-21 tells of the time Jesus was invited to read in the synagogue on the Sabbath in his home town of Nazareth. He read from the scroll of Isaiah that prophesied the coming of the Messiah. After he finished reading, Jesus said in verse 21, 'Today this Scripture has been fulfilled in your hearing.'

Jesus really said two very important things with that statement. The first was that Isaiah was Scripture or the Word of God. In other words Jesus was telling us that the Old Testament was from God. And the second was that he, Jesus, was God's Son, the Messiah, the one God had promised to send to save his people. Jesus was speaking with the authority of God himself.

The New Testament

So how come we needed more books in the Bible? Surely thirty-nine would be enough! But God still had more to say to his people centred on the life and work of his son Jesus. So he inspired more people to write the Gospels (Matthew, Mark, Luke and John), the history of the early church (Acts of the Apostles) and letters of instruction and encouragement (Romans, 1 and 2 Corinthians, Galatians, Ephesians, Philippians, Colossians, 1 and 2 Thessalonians, 1 and 2 Timothy, Titus, Philemon, Hebrews, James, 1 and 2 Peter, 1 and 2 and 3 John and Jude). Finally he gave the Apostle John a prophetic vision of Heaven and the end times which he wrote down in the book of Revelation.

As had happened with the Old Testament books, these books and letters were read out to the early Christians who gathered together to worship God on the first day of the week. Copies were carefully made so that the churches in each city could have their own. However, these were not the only books and letters written after Jesus had risen from the dead and returned to heaven. There were other good books that tried to encourage the early Christians in much the same way Christian books do today. But that didn't mean they should be part of God's Word, the Bible. So the early church had some careful work to do. They had to determine which books should be part of the Canon of the New Testament and which should not. But how to decide?

Let's take a moment and look at some of the history of the church itself. The early church first met in people's homes or in an open place like near the river in Philippi, where Paul and Silas met with Lydia and other believers in Acts 16. Later, when the Roman emperors decided that Christianity was dangerous to the empire and began to put Christians in prison or kill them, the Christians had to meet in secret. Some of them still met in homes, others met in caves or other places they thought the soldiers would not find them. It was a very difficult time to be a Christian. It also meant that the Scriptures had to be carried from place to place and kept in hiding. Some early churches had some of the books while other churches had other books. Because of the danger, it was difficult for any of the small churches to be in touch with each other.

The persecution of Christians finally came to an end in 313 A.D. when the Emperor Constantine issued a law that said Christians were free to worship God and that all those who had taken property belonging to Christians must return it. Of course, it took time for the society to make that change, but eventually Christians were allowed to start building churches. Church leaders known as Presbyters or Bishops began to meet together in councils to make decisions about how the church should be run. They also discussed what should be in the Canon of the New Testament.

In 325 A.D. the First Council of Nicaea met in the city of Nicaea which is in present day Turkey. This was the first time that the church leaders had been able to meet together since the Council of Jerusalem, which you can read about in Acts 15. There was much to discuss, especially since there were some church leaders who were not teaching correctly about who Jesus is. One young man called Athanasius attended the council as Bishop Alexander's assistant. Athanasius was a deacon in the church of Alexandria in Egypt and a student of Bishop Alexander. He was around twenty years old and a fervent Christian. He was anxious to see and hear what the church leaders would discuss and decide. And little did he or any of the church leaders know how important this Council would be to the church and Athanasius himself.

What, no Paper?

As the need for writing materials increased, so did the need for other mediums to write on. When God told his prophets to write down his Words for the people to read and hear, they used scrolls.

Scrolls were made of two types of material: papyrus or parchment. Papyrus was made from a large reed plant of the same name that grew by rivers, especially the River Nile. After the thick stems were cut down, the outer green part was stripped off because it was the inner fibres the papyrus maker needed. He laid strips of these white fibres out on a flat surface horizontally. Then he took another layer and laid it crossways. The moisture from the plant was sticky, so as the strips were pressed together and then dried in the sun, they formed an even page to write on. If they needed more than one sheet, then dried pages were glued side by side to form a scroll. However you could only use one side for writing, the crossways one, because the other side was too bumpy. Papyrus rolled easily and made good scrolls, which were stored in long tubes with the author's name on it. However, while papyrus was rather easy to make and store, not to mention light to carry, it was only a matter of time before the supply of papyrus plants would run out.

What else could people write on? Parchment was the solution. With lots of sheep, goats and cows about, the ancient inventor had the idea to use their skins. Once the animal had been butchered for food, then the skins would be washed first in clear water and then in limewater to remove any flesh or hair. The cleaned skin was stretched out on a frame to dry and finally smoothed with a pumice stone. This is what the Old

Testament books were first written on. When copying out the texts, a scribe could correct his writing errors by using a sponge, much easier and neater than scoring out or even starting again on a new piece. The writing was done in columns, rather than straight across the large hide. The scribe could also write on both sides, providing double the space that papyrus offered. Once the ink dried the parchment was rolled around a rod and then covered with cloth. They were usually stored horizontally in long pigeonhole shelves.

The Wells of Salvation
A.D. 325-367

Athanasius pulled on his cincture to hitch up his dragging alb and shifted the heavy leather bag that he was carrying. He had almost tripped trying to keep up with Bishop Alexander as he hurried along the cobble-stoned street. The Council was about to begin for the day and Bishop Alexander didn't want to miss a single minute. Neither did Athanasius.

They had travelled all the way from Alexandria in northern Egypt to the city of Nicaea[1] for this important meeting of all the church leaders in the known world. Three hundred bishops and their deacons or assistants had arrived days ago filling the city's inns to capacity. Athanasius didn't mind the crowded sleeping arrangements or even the food that was so different from Egyptian meals. He was just glad that Bishop Alexander had included him in the travel party. He barely noticed all the magnificent buildings or the large blue lake the city sat beside. His only thought was on the stone church where they gathered each day to discuss important

---

[1] Nicaea is in modern Turkey and is now called Iznik. See map on page 227.

matters for the church. Today was the beginning of the most important matter of all.

As the two men approached the huge grey stone church the double wooden doors stood open. Bishop Alexander paused to straighten his alb with silk borders and looked back at his deacon.

'Are you ready, my son?' the Bishop inquired.

Athanasius nodded vigorously and hitched up the bag of writing materials once more. Together they entered the church.

Athanasius shivered in the cold air. Even though it was moderately warm outside, the thick stone walls had not allowed much heat in. He had a brief stab of longing for the hot climate of Egypt as he followed Bishop Alexander to his assigned chair and his own stool behind. The church was noisy as all the men gathered; finding their own chairs set around the open perimeter of the church in between the large round pillars that held up the vaulted ceiling. Sunlight poured in from rounded arched windows high up on the walls. At the far end on a raised platform sat the emperor's representative dressed in rich robes. Once decisions had finally been made, the Emperor Constantine himself would attend to hear the consensus of the bishops.

Slowly the conversations and scraping of chairs on the stone floor ceased and Eusebius, Bishop of Nicomedia, rose and unrolled a large scroll. He cleared his throat loudly and then began to read out a set of charges against Bishop Arius. He spoke slowly and clearly for all to hear that Arius was accused of not teaching proper doctrine about Jesus. Arius was telling people that Jesus was not fully God, but rather an inferior divine person who was less than God himself. Many heads began to shake with disapproval, many beards stroked in anger. Jesus was God's Son. He was fully God and fully human.

When Eusebius finished reading he paused and looked around the room. Even from where Athanasius sat on his stool he could see Eusebius' face was full of anger. He expected to hear Eusebius start to lecture Presbyter Arius about his error. Instead, Eusebius took the scroll in both his hands, lifted it high, and tore it in two. Everyone in the church gasped.

After a moment of stunned silence, Athanasius watched in amazement as Arius confidently rose to his feet to defend himself, arguing that he was right and the rest of them were wrong. Athanasius looked around the room. A few bishops nodded their heads in agreement! Now his amazement turned to anger. How could these men of God not see how wrong Arius' views of Jesus really were? Jesus was God's Son. How Athanasius longed to be able to stand up and take part in the debate, but he was not allowed. Only bishops could speak at the Council. As a deacon it was his job to take notes for Bishop Alexander or hand him any scrolls he might want to consult.

To Athanasius' relief most of the bishops began to speak against Arius and his teachings. Bishop Nicholas, sitting close by the offending bishop, rose to speak at the same time Arius stood up again to argue a point. Arius turned to Nicholas and slapped him on the face and told him to sit down. Athanasius jumped to his feet and would have rushed forward and slapped Arius himself if Bishop Alexander had not grabbed hold of his alb.

'Sit down,' Alexander ordered. 'You must not behave as he does.'

Still angry, but sorry to have upset his bishop, Athanasius obeyed. He sat rigidly on his stool; his hands clasped together, he listened in furious silence.

At the end of the day the emperor's representative closed the meeting. The debate was still raging, but everyone was tired and hungry. They would meet to begin again in the morning.

Athanasius could barely contain himself as he walked back to the inn with Bishop Alexander. It seemed to be taking too long to make the best decision.

'Why don't all the bishops just agree and send Arius packing?' Athanasius asked.

'Because this is very important. Who we believe Jesus to be is at the very heart of Christianity. We must proceed carefully, giving complete answers from the Scriptures to everything that Bishop Arius is teaching. We must prove without doubt that he is wrong so that every bishop and priest will know the right doctrines to teach. This is too important to be hurried.'

Athanasius felt impatient with the older man, but because he loved Alexander as a father he kept his thoughts to himself. Over the next few weeks Athanasius watched and listened, working hard to keep himself from leaping up with his own opinions. In the end, Arius was defeated. The Council took a vote and only two bishops sided with Arius. The rest, even angry Eusebius, had all realised that to believe what Arius taught was to deny that Jesus was God's son. The Council drew up a creed[2], stating what all Christians should believe and teach. Athanasius left the Council meeting that day rejoicing and praising God for giving the bishops wisdom and preserving the church from heresy.

At the end of the month-long Council meeting Athanasius and Bishop Alexander returned home to Alexandria and their usual routine. Athanasius was both a student of the bishop and a deacon in the church. As a student he continued his studies in philosophy and theology, learning much from Alexander. As a deacon he was busy assisting the bishop in worship services by reading from the Scriptures and helping dispense the elements of communion. He also visited members of the congregation, enjoying fellowship with them and teaching the children. Three years passed quickly and then Bishop Alexander died.

Athanasius mourned the loss of his friend and teacher. Alexander had been his wise, spiritual father, teaching him the things of God.

---

[2] This creed became known as the Nicene Creed.

Other people were impressed with how Alexander had taught Athanasius, and when the bishops came together to discuss who should take Alexander's place, Athanasius was chosen. Athanasius was honoured and promised to do his best to serve God and his church. But not everyone was happy with the choice.

A group of people within the Egyptian church still supported Arius and his wrong teaching about Jesus. They began stirring up trouble in the churches causing some to say that Athanasius should be replaced with a bishop they chose. When none of the church leaders would listen to them they decided to make trouble for Athanasius himself.

First, they levelled charges of unjust taxes. They claimed Athanasius tried to tax the people of Alexandria to raise money for fancy furniture for the church. Then they complained that Athanasius treated those who believed Arian teachings unjustly, putting them in prison and having them beaten. And, finally, they accused him of murdering Bishop Arsenius, who had recently disappeared.

All of these accusations made Athanasius angry. He wanted to spend his time serving God and his people. Instead he had to leave the city of Alexandria and appear before the synod in the city of Tyre to answer the charges. And who was there to help out Athanasius' enemies? Eusebius of Nicomedia, who really hadn't changed his mind about the heretical Arian teachings after all. But Athanasius didn't come unprepared. He entered the city of Tyre with forty-eight other bishops who supported him. People gathered in the narrow stone streets to see the parade of churchmen, knowing that an important synod meeting was about to take place. Some even cheered to show Athanasius their support.

Once the bishops had assembled in a large church, trumpets sounded outside. Everyone stood as the emperor's representative entered.

'Make way for Count Dionysius, Protector to the Council,' a voice sounded.

The Count entered with a train of assistants and servants, nodded to the bishops and took his seat on a throne set up on a platform at one end of the church. He looked around seriously at the bishops as they too took their seats and called the synod meeting to order. Then he nodded to Eusebius to read out the charges against Athanasius.

When Eusebius finished, Athanasius immediately rose to his feet. He was anxious to speak and prove he was innocent of the charges.

'Brethren, these accusations are monstrous!' his voice echoed off the stone walls. 'These are heinous crimes. Let me answer them and prove my innocence.'

Athanasius paused for effect and then turned to his deacon. The deacon rose and walked to the main door and stood by it.

'Brethren, first to the most serious of the charges: they say I murdered a fellow bishop and cut off his hand to keep in a jar. No such jar was found in my house in Alexandria. They say, then where is Arsenius? He has vanished and you, Athanasius, must have killed him. Malicious, foolish people! Where is Arsenius? Behold!' Athanasius swung around and pointed to the door. His deacon pulled it open.

Everyone looked and saw Bishop Arsenius standing on the stone porch held in place by a sturdy-looking young man. The deacon then took Arsenius' other arm and both men conducted the 'missing' bishop through the gathered churchmen to stand before Count Dionysius.

'Who are you?' the Count asked.

'Arsenius,' came the quiet answer from the ashamed-looking man.

'Did you agree to this deception?'

'Yes, but I bitterly regret it. I wish to repent of my actions and ask forgiveness,' Arsenius replied.

'That will be for your fellow churchmen to decide,' the Count said. 'But I will declare the murder charge has been dropped. There can be no murder when the man in question stands before us.'

Athanasius smiled broadly and looked over at Eusebius. Eusebius glared back and leapt to his feet.

'What about the other charges?' he demanded.

'I was just getting to those,' Athanasius answered. 'I didn't level any taxes on the Alexandrian people. I don't have the power to do that, or to interfere with grain shipments. Those are government duties, not mine. I'm just a poor bishop in a private position.'

'You, poor!' Eusebius shouted. 'You're the bishop of a great city and have much power among the people there. You have misused your influence, persuading people to rebel against the emperor.'

'I have not! You can prove no such thing?' Athanasius shouted back.

'Order! Order!' Count Dionysius called out as more shouting erupted between Eusebius' followers and Athanasius' friends.

Athanasius subsided, recalling the words of Bishop Alexander years before: 'You must not behave as he does.' Athanasius knew his temper was getting the better of him.

But Eusebius carried on. 'He has also misused his power to persecute and imprison those who support Arius and his teaching. I have heard stories of pain and suffering from the poor souls myself. All at Athanasius' command!'

Once more Athanasius leapt to his feet, his temper boiling up again. 'The church councils have ruled that Arian teachings are heretical. If the Arians won't stop teaching then I must put them in prison. How else do I protect the congregation that God has given me to care for?'

More outbursts were heard around the church until the Count cut off all debate and called for silence.

Once order was restored the Count rose to speak. 'There appears to be some case to answer about the abuse of power.

Athanasius, you don't have the right to act as a civil judge. Putting people in prison is not the church's responsibility, regardless of the charges. This meeting is at an end today. We will convene again tomorrow.'

Athanasius called his deacon to him to quickly pick up all their belongings and follow him out of the church. As he made for the door, numerous bishops told him they supported him, but a good many turned away from him too.

'I must get away from here,' he said urgently to his deacon as they walked back to their inn. 'I won't get a fair hearing here. I'll go to Emperor Constantine himself and appeal my case.'

'But how?' the deacon asked. 'You must be invited to see the emperor. Won't he be angry that you haven't listened to the Count, his representative?'

'I'll take that chance. We must leave immediately, so no one will notice we have gone until tomorrow morning.'

The deacon wasn't happy but he agreed. At the inn, Athanasius quickly threw some items in a cloth bag and picked up his chasuble. He handed some coins to the deacon to pay for the room, while he went to the stable to get the horses.

It was a long journey. For safety, Athanasius and his deacon joined a caravan of traders and merchants heading to the great city Constantinople on the Black Sea. In the midst of all the men, animals and wagons, they were able to keep to themselves. They travelled all day and then circled into a group for safety at night. They shared in the food by paying their share and then Athanasius would go off to a quiet place to pray. He prayed for safety and strength and most of all prayed for courage to explain the truth to the emperor.

As the caravan drew near to Constantinople, Athanasius began to pray for an opportunity to secure an audience with the emperor. To his amazement, God answered almost immediately. The gates of the city opened and the emperor himself rode out on his horse, followed by a few bodyguards. They swung off the road and through a meadow by the walls. Athanasius seized his opportunity. He turned his horse to follow the emperor across the meadow. He stopped a short distance from the riding party and called out to the emperor, who turned his head when he heard his name. One of the bodyguards immediately galloped over to Athanasius.

'Who are you and what do you want?' the soldier challenged.

Athanasius sat up straight and said, 'I am Athanasius, Bishop of Alexandria, here to plead for justice.'

The guard relayed the message to the emperor and Athanasius was beckoned forward. Constantine, a strong, seasoned warrior, sat on his horse and waited as Athanasius dismounted and bowed low.

'Well? I thought you were answering the charges in Tyre. What are you doing here?' the emperor demanded.

'Your Majesty,' Athanasius replied. 'I have been wrongly accused and can get no justice there. I appeal to you to hear my case yourself.'

'Very well, but do it quickly. I had hoped for a few minutes of peaceful exercise instead of yet another problem to solve.'

So Athanasius explained how his enemies were trying to disturb the church and allow heresy to be taught. 'They think if they can remove me from the church, they will be able to do as they please. I must contend for the truth, I must be faithful to God. Please hear the case yourself. Call the bishops here and be the judge.'

'I think *you* are the disturber of the peace. I've heard the charges and Eusebius has argued them well enough for me. But I will listen yet again and whatever I decide you will obey.'

Athanasius bowed low as the emperor turned his horse and rode off with his guards.

Sadly, in the end the emperor preferred to listen to Eusebius and the Arians, and Athanasius found himself banished from his home and his church. But he refused to stop fighting for the truth. He went to see one of the emperor's sons, also called Constantine. This Constantine agreed that the Arian doctrines were wrong and he allowed Athanasius to live in his household.

A few years later in 337, Emperor Constantine died and his three sons split the kingdom between them. Constantine II urged his brothers to let Athanasius return to his position of Bishop of Alexandria and they finally agreed. However, all was not well in Alexandria. The Arians had appointed a new bishop in Athanasius' place and he wasn't moving. The Christians of Alexandria were upset that Athanasius, whom they had known and loved since he was a deacon, was not allowed to return. Once more Athanasius had to seek help. This time he went to Bishop Julius in Rome, someone that the emperors listened to. But the wrangling took several years. It came down to a fight between the Arians and those who believed the Nicene Creed. Whenever he could, Athanasius spoke or wrote about the importance of right doctrine, encouraging the church leaders not to give in to Arian beliefs that denied that Jesus was the Son of God. At last the Arians were defeated and after seven years of exile, Athanasius was reinstalled as bishop.

As Athanasius rode into his home city, the people streamed out of their homes to greet him. He waved as they shouted and sang songs of praise to God. Boats filled the Nile delta with even more people. The whole city rejoiced for days with banquets and services of thanksgiving. How glad Athanasius was to be with the people of God and ministering to them.

For ten years he remained there carrying out his duties in the church, training deacons and visiting his flock. However, God still had something more he wanted Athanasius to do. It meant more trouble, but also great blessing.

One of the brother emperors, Constantius, had been won over by the Arian doctrines and he decided he must see that all bishops agreed with Arian beliefs or be deposed. Once more Athanasius had to fight to protect the church and God's Word. He spoke out loudly against this emperor's plan and soon he had to face the consequences.

On a Sunday when Athanasius was leading the people in worship in the huge church in Alexandria, five thousand soldiers arrived and surrounded the church. The worship stopped and people looked to their bishop to tell them what to do. Athanasius calmly went to his chair near the altar and sat down. He called to one of the deacons to lead the congregation in singing Psalm 136. Soon the noise of the marching soldiers outside was drowned out by the hundreds of raised voices inside.

The deacon sang: 'O thank the Lord, for he is good.'
The people sang in reply: 'His mercy endures forever.'
'Thanks to the God of gods give ye.'
'His mercy endures forever.'

And so the Psalm went on with the people singing the refrain after each stanza. It heartened them all so that they stood strong when the soldiers broke through the heavy wooden doors and began to push their way in. The people purposely blocked the soldiers to slow their progress toward their beloved bishop. In anger, the soldiers pushed harder against the crowd and began using their weapons. A riot was in danger of breaking out. In the confusion the deacons were able to sneak Athanasius out another door, past the soldiers and to freedom. But Athanasius couldn't stay in Alexandria without the soldiers finding him. So friends found a boat and took Athanasius down the River Nile and then out into the desert to a monastery. The monks gladly took him in and hid him from the emperor's soldiers.

At first Athanasius was angry. Why couldn't people see the truth that was taught in the Scriptures? Why did they believe the heretical Arian doctrines? And he was getting tired of fighting. He had been a faithful bishop for almost thirty years and still some could not stop troubling the church with these heresies.

'Maybe that's why you are here,' one of the monks suggested after listening to Athanasius complain. 'Maybe God has given you this time away from all the difficulties to rest.'

'Rest! How can I rest when my congregation now has a bishop who is really a wolf in sheep's clothing! I need to protect the people from error.'

Another monk shrugged. 'So do that. You don't need to be there to teach them.'

Athanasius looked confused for a minute and then smiled. 'Of course. I could write a book about God's truth. Explain the Christian doctrines clearly for people to read or have read to them.'

Athanasius remained in hiding at the desert monastery for six years and in that time he wrote several books. In his book entitled *Orations* Athanasius explained, using Scripture, the importance of knowing Jesus as God's son, equal with God in every way. The books were copied and taken into the cities and distributed to those who could read. Even though God had removed Athanasius from the debates of the synods and councils of the church, his books were used to help explain the truth and eventually to defeat the Arians in 359. Then Athanasius was invited back to a welcoming Alexandria to finish out his life as their bishop.

As Athanasius settled back into Alexandria he thought about his time in the monastery. He now realised that God had set him aside for those years for a reason. While the fight for the truth was important, it was equally important that Athanasius himself not neglect the study of God's Word. He had time to study, pray and reflect on the Scriptures without distractions. To be a good church leader he had to keep reading God's Word so he could remain strong in the truth. In fact, all Christians needed to read and study God's Word. And they needed to know which books were actually the inspired Word of God. Many Christians had written books since the apostles' time, over three centuries ago, but those books weren't inspired. So in 367 Athanasius decided to write a pastoral letter to all the churches in Egypt to be read out when the people gathered for worship at Easter.

'Dearly beloved in the Lord', he wrote. 'Now that the heretics have been dealt with we must make sure that we do not fall into error ourselves. There are some who have tried to include writings other than divinely inspired Scripture in the Canon. So I will be clear. Only the apostles who from the beginning were eye-witnesses to our Lord were divinely inspired to write the books of the New Testament. Here is a list of those books, handed down and accredited as divine, for all to know.'

Athanasius listed all the books of the Old Testament from Genesis through to Malachi. Then he began a list of the New Testament books, twenty-seven in all from Matthew to Revelation. He concluded his letter with these words:

'These are the wells of salvation, so that he who thirsts may be satisfied with the sayings in these. Let no one add to these. Let nothing be taken away.'

Living in a Monastery:

A monastery was, and still is, a community of men who have chosen to live together for the purpose of serving God. (Women, called nuns, had their own monasteries, also called convents.) That is not to say that the rest of us don't serve God in our everyday lives, but monks and nuns had a specific way of living in mind. Taking the verses in Paul's letter to the Corinthian church where he suggested that unmarried people could serve God better without the distractions of a family, the monks chose to live in a separate community and devote their time and energy solely to prayer, studying God's Word and helping others in need. They made promises called vows that they would stay in the monastery, obey all the rules and give themselves up completely to serving God. But monks weren't lazy layabouts. Their lives were busy and by our modern standards exhausting.

Their day started at 3 a.m. They went to church to pray together and sing psalms of praise. In fact throughout their day they were in church ten times for short services of singing and praying until they went to bed around 8 p.m. In between those times they had other things to do. They ate two meals a day, or sometimes only one, of simple foods like cheese, bread and fish and they drank weak beer. There was no talking during meals. Instead, someone read from the Bible or other religious works. They attended chapter meetings where the abbot reminded them of the rules and issued punishments to those who had broken them. During the work times, everyone had a job to do, and they were expected to do it cheerfully to honour God. Some went to the scriptorium to study or make books. Some went to various places like the refectory (kitchen and dining area), the church or store houses, all of which needed to be cleaned and kept tidy. Some monks taught the novices, young men and boys who had come to study in the monastery school. A large monastery might also have a guest house for travellers or a hospital to care for the sick, and these too were run by the monks. And some monks were chosen to distribute food and used clothing to the poor. Not a moment was wasted in using their time and energy to serve God.

From the Canon
to Translating

Athanasius died in A.D. 373, six years after he wrote his pastoral letter on the Canon of the Bible. Other bishops, too, thought it was important to set the Canon. Finally, at the Council of Hippo in 393, the matter was closed. The church, with the help of the Holy Spirit, now recognised as inspired[1] all the New Testament books outlined in Athanasius' letter. Other books and letters written by early Christians were helpful to read, but were not part of the inspired Word of God. Now the church had the complete Bible with the Old and New Testaments.

During this time a boy named Jerome was born in northern Greece. Jerome, the oldest of three children, was very clever and his parents soon realised that he should have an opportunity to study at the best school in the known world. So in the early 340s, when Jerome was twelve years old, he was sent to Rome with his best friend, Bonosus. Together the young men grew up reading literature, learning languages and studying in the law courts. They

[1] Inspired in this case means that the Bible came from God himself. In 2 Peter 1:19-21 it says that men, chosen by God, were moved by the Holy Spirit to write the Word of God.

both had brilliant futures ahead of them. Who knew where they could end up with the right contacts and their great intellects? But God knew. He had a plan that didn't include fighting lawsuits or working for the emperor and his government.

After they left Rome and followed the emperor's court to Trèves[2], Jerome and Bonosus felt God's call on their lives. Both young men had grown up in Christian homes and loved God, but they had enjoyed their freedom living in the busy city of Rome. They had not lived entirely as they should have and now they were sorry for their sins and asked God to forgive them. Bonosus decided that he should give his life from now on to serving God in a monastery. He would study the Scriptures, pray and help others rather than pleasing himself. Jerome too felt called to be a monk, but he was a restless person. So when he decided to leave the emperor's court, he planned to travel to Palestine and live as a monk there.

Jerome spent many years in a monastery out in the Syrian desert. During that time he wrote books about the Bible and Christian living. Many people read his books and he became recognised as an important Christian writer and thinker.

Then he had an opportunity to return to Rome, a chance he didn't want to miss. And God had a job for Jerome to do.

---

[2] Trèves: a city now called Trier in southwestern Germany on the Moselle River. During the Roman Empire it was considered an imperial city.

The Testy Translator

A.D. 382-405

Jerome, dressed in his monk's rough cloak, stood looking at the city of Rome[1] from a rise in the road and smiled. He thought of the city as his home, even though his family had never lived there. Coming to Rome at the age of twelve, Jerome had spent eight happy years studying with his best friend, Bonosus. Jerome's smile widened to a grin as he thought about the fun they had had together, and what a good travelling companion Bonosus had been when they left Rome as young men to pursue their careers. Jerome shook his head. That was over twenty years ago.

'What are you daydreaming about, my friend? Or are you composing another treatise?' Bishop Paulinus asked with a smile. 'I thought you came on this journey to be our guide in this great city. We can't have you just standing there gazing out into the air with a silly grin on your face.'

Jerome gave a start and turned to face the Greek bishop from Antioch. 'My apologies. Just a few memories from my younger days.'

---

[1] See map on page 227.

Paulinus laughed. 'You're not so old.'

Epiphanius, the Bishop of Salamis, came puffing up the steep incline behind them. 'Why are we waiting? I thought we had arrived at the city. We still need to find Lady Marcella's villa and I'm hungry.'

Paulinus laughed again, but Jerome rounded on the Bishop with a stern look. 'You are in danger of making your belly your god,' he warned.

'Don't quote Scripture at me. And look who seeks to correct a bishop!' Epiphanius snapped back. 'The monk who travels with the largest library I have ever seen. I pity those who have to carry it all!'

'Now, now,' Paulinus intervened. 'Let's go into the city. Epiphanius is right. We do need to find our hostess' home. And then see to our appointments with Pope Damasus.'

The party of bishops, monks and servants made their way along the wide stone road that began to fill with people as they entered through the stone arched gateway. At first Jerome was glad to be home and he walked confidently through the streets. But he quickly became distressed to see so many pagan temples standing so close to Christian churches. The buildings were magnificent structures of stone and marble, but still pagan. And the noise of so many people jostling one another and vendors calling out their wares was louder than he remembered.

At last they arrived at Lady Marcella's villa. They were ushered through the gate and into the atrium featuring a large fountain and stone benches. They were invited to sit while slaves removed their sandals and washed their dusty, tired feet. Lady Marcella, a wealthy widow, arrived to welcome them just as the slaves had finished their duties.

Jerome nodded approvingly. Marcella was modestly dressed in a sleeveless dark linen stola, her dark hair covered with a veil[1] that fell around her shoulders. Unlike most wealthy women, she wore no make-up or jewellery.

'You must be tired and hungry after your long journey,' she said with a smile. 'I've prepared a meal for you.'

They were then led into an inner room with a table full of good food and couches to sit or recline on to eat. Jerome was less impressed with this. 'This is more than we need,' he muttered.

---

[1] The veil covered only the hair and not the face.

Lady Marcella heard him and agreed. 'Yes, but when you have finished I have others to feed too. Nothing will be wasted,' she assured him. And she was true to her word. Jerome learned later that she fed her family and household servants and then the rest was given to the poor.

Several days later as Jerome was leaving the villa to go with the bishops to see Pope Damasus, a group of women arrived. Lady Marcella welcomed them and then turned to explain to Jerome.

'Lady Paula and her daughter, and some of our friends, often join me to study the Scriptures. Should you have some time later, we would appreciate you answering some of our questions. You have written many good books and we think you could help us understand the Bible better.'

Jerome smiled. 'Of course I would. It's so good to see women spending their time studying the Holy Books. Please let me know when you will meet again and I will arrange to be there.'

He bowed to the women and then went to lead his bishops out through the busy city to the Basilica of St Peter. When they entered the large atrium full of marble columns they were met by a young deacon and taken to the pope's residence. The elderly Bishop of Rome beckoned them forward to his ornate chair where he sat. He greeted Paulinus and Epiphanius and then turned to Jerome.

'I have heard a lot about you, Jerome,' Pope Damasus said. 'I'm in need of a secretary. With your ability to understand so many languages you could help with my letters and documents.'

Jerome bowed to the pope, feeling very pleased. 'I would be most honoured,' he replied.

'Very well, my son, there is no time like the present to begin. My deacon here will take you to the secretary's office. You will find many letters and documents there. Please sort them in order of date and importance and I will come and meet with you after I have seen the good bishops here.'

And so Jerome began his new job, and soon found it was very demanding. First he dealt with the backlog of correspondence and then met with Damasus regularly to receive instructions on the new letters or treatises that needed preparing. While Latin was the principal language used in Rome, Damasus also corresponded with the Greek and Egyptian bishops. So Jerome spent his time translating documents for them. He was given a staff of young deacons to write out the final copies to be sent.

When Jerome was not occupied with his new job, he met with the women at Marcella's home to teach them about the Bible. Jerome was amazed at how much the women had read of the Scriptures. They worked hard to understand the text written in older Latin[2], but were full of questions about what it all meant. Jerome was only too glad to answer them. How good it was to see people hungry for God's Word.

One day after they had finished discussing the day's work, Pope Damasus said to Jerome, 'My son, I have been thinking for some time that we really need to start a translation project on the New Testament books. They were all written in Greek long ago, but most people now speak Latin. The Latin translation we have now is poor. Would you be willing to begin making a new Latin translation?'

Jerome didn't hesitate for a moment. 'Yes! That is exactly what the church needs now. I'm leading a group of women in studying the Bible. It would be so much easier if it were in the everyday language they speak.'

Jerome began work that very afternoon. He knew it would take several years to complete all twenty-seven books and he also

---

[2] Older Latin would be like us reading the King James Version of the Bible. Like Lady Marcella, we can read the English words very well, but sometimes the different sentence structure or even vocabulary makes it difficult to understand.

knew that this gave him an even greater opportunity to learn the deeper meanings in the Scriptures. Jerome was thrilled with this new challenge and a chance to work with languages, although he still had to balance this project with his other work for Damasus and his Bible study group at Marcella's home. The next two years were very busy indeed.

Translating the New Testament was tedious work sometimes, looking for just the right word in Latin that conveyed the same meaning as the Greek word. Jerome was very careful to get it right because this was God's Word. Sometimes his eyes hurt after long hours of poring over the handwritten Greek Bible. Once he had finished, he had professional scribes copy out the translation in as neat a manuscript as possible. Then Jerome checked it for any transcription errors and declared it finished.

In 384, Pope Damasus suddenly died and Jerome found himself without a job, although he was still working on the translation. After the pope died, Jerome found living in Rome less comfortable. Because he had worked for the pope, people had been polite to him, even when he preached sermons against some of the Christians' extravagant lifestyles. But now those same people began to turn away from Jerome, refusing to have him in their homes and making nasty comments about him. The only place that was still comfortable for him was at Lady Marcella's home, studying the Scriptures with Paula and her daughter, Eustochium, and other godly women. One evening, after they had finished reading part of Paul's letter to the Philippians, Jerome made an announcement.

'I have decided to leave Rome. I find the worldliness of the Christian community here too much to accept. Few spend their time studying the Scriptures or live as simply as you women do. I'd rather go somewhere else where the Christian community will be more unified.'

'Where?' Paula asked, worried about losing her spiritual advisor. 'How can you leave us here?'

'I'd like to go back to Palestine. I was able to learn the Hebrew language the last time I lived there, which made studying the Old Testament books easier. At some point I plan to translate the whole Bible into Latin and that would be the best place to do it. I also want to start a monastery there, a place where men can live, and pray and study God's Word.'

'How wonderful! To live in the place where Jesus lived.' Paula exclaimed. 'How I would love to go too.'

'Why don't we?' her daughter, Eustochium, asked. 'We have no ties here in Rome. You told me you want to remain a widow, and I don't plan to marry anyone. I'd rather live in the type of community Jerome is talking about. We could start a monastery for women.'

Paula nodded thoughtfully. 'Your father left us a great deal of money when he died. We could use that money to pay for the trip and build the monastery we would need. That way we wouldn't need to be dependent on anyone. What do you think, Jerome?'

Jerome nodded enthusiastically. 'That's a wonderful idea. Would any of you other ladies be able to join Paula and her daughter?'

Marcella shook her head sadly. 'I like the idea, but I have an elderly mother I must care for. However, my husband also left me more money than I can possibly use. So let me give you some for the journey and the monastery.'

The other women also declined to go but promised to write letters and pray for their safety.

Jerome then set out to find others who might accompany them to the land of Jesus' birth. By the summer several men and women had agreed and they had a travelling party of over a dozen. They left Rome and travelled a short distance to Ostia where they boarded a ship to sail across the Mediterranean Sea to Palestine. They stopped at the island of Cyprus for a while and then in Antioch to visit with the Christian communities there. Jerome was a well-known preacher and scholar. Many people wanted to hear him preach and ask him questions about interpreting certain passages of the Bible. That started an idea for Jerome. He began to write commentaries on each of the books of the Bible to help answer people's questions.

Once the party arrived in Palestine, Paula requested that before they settled down they tour some of the places mentioned in the Bible.

'I would like to see where God fed Elijah, or the beach where Paul knelt to pray with certain disciples before leaving for his last trip to Jerusalem. And then Jerusalem itself where our Lord was so cruelly treated, and Bethlehem, where he was born.'

Jerome agreed. 'It would add so much more meaning to the biblical stories to see where they actually happened. And while we are still travelling, I think I would also like to go down to Egypt. There is a monastery I would like to visit and ask the monks about how they set up their community.'

Everyone in the group decided to go with Jerome and Paula, even though it was now winter. Cold winds blew and they had to draw their woollen cloaks tightly around them as they rode on donkeys. But Jerome hardly noticed the cold. As they arrived at each new place, Paula would ask him to read to them the biblical story. They stopped by the place Abraham was thought to have buried his wife, Sarah, the well where the Ethiopian man was baptised by the Apostle Philip, and the village of Bethany where Mary and Martha had lived and Jesus had raised Lazarus from the dead.

Each time they stopped at a site Jerome would also seek out the local Jewish people. He would discuss the Hebrew words used in the Old Testament stories, trying to get a clearer understanding of the language. He took notes, planning to use the knowledge he was gaining for his translation project later.

After spending a whole year visiting all the places in Palestine, the entire group set out for Egypt. They decided to travel overland, following the trade routes through the desert where the Israelites had spent forty years. From there they crossed over the Red Sea and into the land of Egypt where they settled in Alexandria for a month. While there Jerome met with biblical scholars and discussed the Scriptures and interpretations. Paula spent some of her time caring for the many poor in the city and sharing her vast wealth. Then, last of all, they journeyed out to the Egyptian desert to the monastery where Athanasius had hidden from the emperor's soldiers twenty-five years earlier.

Dressed in simple monk's robes, the entire group of monks stood outside their humble huts and welcomed Jerome and his travelling party. Jerome was pleased to see his friend, Paula, take a deep interest in how the monastery was run; what did they eat, where did they sleep, when did they pray, what work did they do? Jerome was doing the same thing, taking notes and speaking with the Abbot of the monastery about how to deal with disagreements that arose from time to time among the monks and how to decide who should join the monastery. Not everyone was able to live such a rigorous life. They collected up all these thoughts and ideas to use when they returned to Palestine to set up their own monasteries, one for women and one for men. They would live simply as the monks in Egypt lived, spending no time on comforts beyond basic food and clothing so that they would have more time for Bible study and prayer. What better way to spend one's life here on earth than in prayer with their heavenly Father.

After a short time the travelling party decide to return to Palestine. The return journey took them up the River Nile to Alexandria, where they transferred to a larger ship to cross the Mediterranean Sea to land at Maiuma, a port city near Gaza.

From there they finished the last part of the journey by donkey, finally arriving in the village of Bethlehem.

For the next three years Jerome did little translating. There was too much to do to set up the monasteries. They chose a location near the church that was thought to be built over the place where Jesus was born. It was a lovely area with trees and flowers.

'All these trees will be very useful for building our huts, dining room and chapel,' Jerome observed to his small group of monks. 'We must all pitch in and help, and we will hire some of the local people to do some of the skilled work.'

Across the road Paula was also busy planning her buildings for the women's monastery with some local builders. 'I also want to build a hospital and an inn for travellers. We can help the sick and show hospitality to strangers. I think that is especially important here in Bethlehem where Mary and Joseph were only given a stable to stay in.'

The workmen nodded and asked questions about exactly where she wanted her buildings and how large they were to be. Eustochium, Paula's daughter, took over for her mother to discuss and direct all the details of the construction.

During all this construction, Paula and her small group of women lived in a hostel. Since they couldn't do the actual work that the men did, they spent their time in prayer, Bible study and helping the poor of the village. Many of the people of Bethlehem were either farmers or shepherds. When the crops were good and sheep well fed, the village prospered, but the years of poor crops and sick sheep meant poverty for all. Paula, with her fortune, was able to help many in times of need.

Jerome supervised the women's work, as well as spending time instructing his own group of monks. He preached most Sundays in the church where both men and women gathered for worship. He also preached occasionally in Jerusalem and travelled to Caesarea for a time. When he returned from his travels the monasteries were finally completed.

Jerome gazed with satisfaction at the groups of buildings. On one side of the road stood the men's monastery with its vegetable garden and fig trees. On the other side stood the women's monastery and the hospital, with the traveller's inn a little farther down the way. A flock of sheep wandered into view with their shepherd leading them down the road past the church to the pastures just outside the village. A peaceful place to serve God, Jerome thought. Now would be a good time to start his translation work again, and his commentary series on the books of the Bible.

Sixty-year-old Jerome's eyesight was weak from all the studying and writing he had done during his life. So he needed to have an amanuensis to help him with his new projects. Jerome selected one the monks with a good writing hand and a quick ear, and told him his duties.

'I will dictate what I want you to write. You must only write what I say. No adding your own comments. Sometimes I will think very fast. Other times slower. Do you think you can do this?' Jerome looked intently at the young man's face. 'Both projects are very important. It is vital that we are accurate with the translation of the Old Testament. And the commentaries will be used to explain the books of the Bible.'

The young monk nodded eagerly. 'I will do my very best. I'm sure I will learn a great deal about God's Word.'

And so the work began. It was difficult. Jerome tackled some of his New Testament commentary series first. Since he had already translated the New Testament books into Latin, he was able to write the commentaries without too much more study. Jerome and the young monk met in Jerome's study, surround by his huge library that had travelled with him wherever he went. The young monk sat at a wooden table by the window for the best light with his quill pen, ink and parchment ready to take down his master's words. Jerome had another table littered with open books and manuscripts. At times he would sit and read passages from other Christian writings or study the biblical text itself and then begin to dictate. When he got excited about an idea, he would pace back and forth in the room speaking rapidly. His amanuensis wrote furiously to keep pace with the steady flow of words. Some days Jerome dictated as much as a thousand lines for his secretary to record and then re-copy in a neater handwriting.

As the New Testament commentary series was nearing its end, Jerome began to think about his great translation project of the Old Testament. In preparation Jerome had continued his study of the Hebrew language with Baraninas, a Jewish man who lived nearby. Baraninas, afraid of what his fellow Jews would say if they saw him speaking to a Christian monk, chose to arrive at the monastery after dark and meet with Jerome several evenings a week. Jerome had lists of questions as he studied the Hebrew Old Testament and Baraninas helped explain some of the more obscure words and meanings.

At last Jerome felt ready to tackle the project. He decided to start with the books of Samuel and Kings, partly because some folk had been asking for those books to be translated and partly because the history books were easier than the law or the poetry. For fourteen years Jerome worked on the Old Testament, completing the work in A.D. 405 when he was seventy-four years old. He sat back in his chair with satisfaction. Now people had a careful translation of God's Word in their own language of Latin, and it was eventually known as the Vulgate.

From Scrolls to Codex (what's that?)

Imagine you are sitting in a classroom and your teacher says turn to the section on the Peloponnesian Wars in your text. So you start to unroll your scroll, scanning column after column, looking for the required text. Just a little awkward, trying not to hit your neighbour while you search through as much as thirty feet of parchment.

This was the very problem the early scholars had when studying the Scriptures. When Jerome wrote his commentaries on the books of the Bible, he wanted to compare Scripture with Scripture. In other words, as he prepared to write on one part of Scripture, like the crucifixion of Jesus, he wanted to be able to refer to prophecies in Isaiah and the Psalms about the Messiah and his death. So he'd have to get out the scrolls on Isaiah (and there were a lot because the Prophet Isaiah wrote a long book) and unroll each one, searching for all the references he wanted for his commentary. There were no chapter or verse divisions in the Greek, Hebrew or early Latin Bible. It was a very slow, cumbersome way to do research.

So how to make it easier? The first step was to cut the larger parchment pieces into smaller, regular sized portions that held one column of text. Because you could write on both sides of parchment, the author, or copyist, could write the continuous text starting on one side, then the other and carrying on to the next page. Then the pages were sewn together on one side. This form was called a codex, the Latin word that originally meant 'block of wood' but came to mean 'book.' The church is usually given the credit for popularising the use of the codex. While scholars and translators used this form because it made God's Word easier to read, everyone else soon discovered how useful the format was for any book they wanted to read.

Meanwhile all over Europe

A.D. 400 to 850

Jerome lived a long life, dying in A.D. 420 around the age of eighty-eight. Even though he remained in Palestine, Jerome received letters from many friends around the known world who told him of the threats to the Roman Empire. Groups of people from northern Europe were moving south, looking for new lands to conquer. For a time the Roman army was able to hold them back, but in 410 the Goths, led by their king, Alaric, broke through and captured the city of Rome. Many people died, including Jerome's friend, Lady Marcella and her family. Jerome's home town of Stridon had also been wiped out, its lands seized by the invaders and the townspeople scattered.

All over Europe these northern Germanic tribes were on the move, overrunning the borders of the Roman Empire as far away as Britain. Life in the fifth and sixth centuries changed dramatically from the well-ordered society governed by Roman law to the constant fear of raiding parties of warriors arriving to take whatever they wished. Many young people were carried off as slaves, never to see their families again. Many families were forced to give up their land and then pay taxes to the new owners. There were also threats from the south and the east as the followers of Islam began to expand their borders too. Whether they were rich or poor, everyone was in danger.

During those unsettled centuries the church leaders tried to do a number of things. First, they continued to preach and provide comfort to the people by reminding them that God was with them even during troubled times. Secondly, they sent out missionaries throughout Europe. It was a dangerous business being God's messenger to the vicious, pagan warriors who preferred to worship their own gods of war. Some very brave men were martyred when they preached to the warriors. Last of all, the monasteries became the storehouses of books and learning.

In times when people had to be on the move, fighting or running from invaders, there was little time for the usual activities like sending children to school. Learning, which had been highly prized during the Roman Empire, was being lost, except among the monks. As part of their service to God they continued to train their young men to read and write and make books. The book-making consisted of carefully copying out by hand each book they had and then binding it. The task demanded careful, clear writing and absolute accuracy. It took a long time to produce a copy of a book, and it became the monks' primary occupation along with prayer and studying the Scriptures. And the most important book they copied out was the Bible. Safe within the monastery libraries, the Bible was protected from all the warfare around Europe.

However, keeping God's Word safe had also kept people from reading it. By the seventh and eighth centuries most people, including kings and nobles, could not read. They had never been taught. The monks and church leaders were the only ones who could still study God's Word. So the monasteries became the centres of learning, and the monks and priests became the teachers of the people.

In Britain the people had experienced the same upheaval of repeated invasions as the rest of Europe. After four centuries the country had been divided among the various groups of people. The Saxons held much of what we now call England, with the Britons confined to what is now Wales and northwest of England. In the north the Picts and Scots fought for supremacy and in Ireland the Celtic tribes defended their island against all invaders.[1] By the ninth century the country was once again quiet, but it was short-lived. In the 860s the Danes made their first foray into Saxon territory and the fighting began again. A few years before, a young prince had been born in Wessex; Alfred, fifth son of Ethelwulf, King of Wessex. Alfred grew up to be a great warrior and a great king. And God used Alfred to bring God's Word back to the people.

---

[1] See map on page 228.

The King calls for a Translator

A.D. 878-899

'Alfred is alive!'

'The king has returned!'

The news travelled rapidly from village to village throughout Wessex[1]. The Saxon people had feared their king was dead, killed by Guthrum and his Danish army when they had launched a surprise attack during the Christmas celebrations the year before. Now five months later, as the spring flowers filled the hillsides, hope returned to the fearful people. God had kept their king safely hidden on the Isle of Athelney.

As the news spread thanes and churls began to gather once more, bringing their shields, swords, spears and metal helmets. They streamed in from Somerset, Wiltshire and Hampshire to meet King Alfred in the shade of the forest edge at Selwood. Coming from his exile, Alfred was dressed in a shabby dark blue three-quarter length tunic and trousers. His leather boots were worn and muddy. The only clue to his kingship was the large

---

[1] England was not a united country at this time. It was made up of several smaller kingdoms.

jewelled pin that fastened his deep red cloak to his right shoulder. His shoulder-length dark hair hung down his shoulders, coming even with his bushy beard.

Alfred greeted his rallying troops with relief. His greatest fear had been that the Danes had so thoroughly defeated his people that they couldn't fight again. Now he saw their joy and excitement as they gathered about him waiting to hear his battle plan, and it buoyed him up too. Victory might well be within their grasp.

'It's time to deal with Guthrum and his army once and for all,' Alfred began. 'They are camped at Chippenham. Between here and there are the Wiltshire Downs, the place where we will defeat them. We go in on foot, using our shield walls and our weapons. We must go in with purpose and pray that God gives us the day. Guthrum is mighty, but God is mightier still.'

The men cheered and banged their round wooden shields with their swords or spears. They were ready for battle, and the march to the plains began.

Guthrum had scouts set up around the area and he soon received word that Alfred was advancing with a mighty army. He too called his soldiers together and went out to meet the Saxons. The battle raged on for hours, the air full of the sounds of clashing swords, clanging shields and cries of pain and death. Many soldiers fell on each side, but slowly Alfred and the Saxons gained the upper hand. Finally Guthrum himself called for his Danes to retreat, and they turned and ran from the field. Alfred called out the order to follow the enemy and capture their leader.

Covered in sweat and blood, the Saxons gained on the Danes, killing some and forcing the rest to take refuge in the fortified town of Chippenham. Alfred set his soldiers to surround the town and penned them in. For fourteen days the Saxons held siege on the Danes, until, without water and food, the Danes surrendered.

'Shall we kill them all?' one thane asked eagerly.

'No!' Alfred replied. 'There will be no more killing. We've had enough bloodshed. Find Guthrum and bring him to me. Guard the rest and let none escape.'

Alfred turned and walked a little way from his army. He prayed as he walked that what he planned to do was the wisest course of action. Ever since he became king he had been fighting Danes, as his father and brothers had before him. Alfred wanted to see an end to it if he could.

The mighty Dane leader was brought and forced to kneel before Alfred. His fur pelt tunic was matted with dirt, as were his long blond braids of hair. He looked as tired as Alfred felt.

'Get up,' Alfred said quietly. 'We need to talk. Come with me.'

Puzzled, Guthrum slowly rose to his feet, looking about to see if there was a trick involved. Then he followed Alfred a few yards away from the other men.

'I want peace between us,' Alfred began.

Grudgingly Guthrum nodded. 'You have killed many of my best warriors and we have no supplies to sustain us here. We too want peace. What are your terms? Do you want my sons as hostages?'

'No, I have something else in mind. I want two things. First, you and your family must agree to stop worshipping your pagan gods and become Christians. Second, you will leave Wessex altogether. You have Mercia, stay there and I will recognise the boundary between us. You rule there and I will rule here.' Alfred folded his arms across his chest and waited for Guthrum to reply.

The burley Dane was astonished. Then slowly he smiled and nodded. 'Yes, this is good. We will do as you ask, but you must teach us what Christians believe. We do not know your religion.'

Alfred smiled broadly and extended his hand to his enemy turned friend. They grasped each other's forearms to seal the agreement.

The next day Alfred called for a contract to be written out with the terms of the peace. As the warriors from both sides gathered round Alfred commanded that the contract be read out. Alfred then took a quill pen and wrote his name. Guthrum, unable to read or write, made a mark with the pen to show his acceptance.

Over the next few months the boundaries were clearly set so that the Danes settled in Mercia and the Saxons remained in Wessex. And according to the peace agreement, Alfred sent a priest to instruct Guthrum and his sons in the Christian faith. Then, true to his word, Guthrum and his sons were baptised, along with thirty of his warriors. Alfred himself attended and stood as godfather to

Guthrum and his sons. He welcomed them into God's family and gave them gifts to celebrate the occasion.

Alfred had a great deal to do once peace was assured in his kingdom. Because of the chaos and uncertainty that war brings, many of the villages and towns were in disrepair. Many fields had been left unplanted and food was short. And there was little regard for law keeping. Everyone looked out for his own rights, even if it meant his neighbours suffered.

Alfred called together his Witan in the King's Hall, a large barn-sized wooden house. In the centre of the hall a warm fire glowed in a fire pit surrounded with large rocks. The smoke rose up and out of the building through a hole in the thatched roof directly above the fire. Alfred, dressed in tunic and trousers of fine red wool and a simple gold crown upon his head, sat on an armed chair at one end of the room. Around him sat his thanes and a few bishops on wooden benches. They had already enjoyed a meal of roast chicken and beef, bread and honeyed mead, the remains of which were being cleared away from the trestle tables by servants. Everyone was in good spirits.

'We have much work to do,' Alfred began. 'First, we need to discuss our defences.'

'Has Guthrum been threatening to break the treaty?' one tall blond Saxon thane asked. 'We'll soon see to him.' Others around him nodded and murmured their assent.

'Guthrum is holding to his side of the treaty,' Alfred assured them. 'However, we have spent so many years fighting each other that all the churls have gone back to rebuild their homes and plant their fields. They don't want to be part of a fyrd anymore, and I understand why. But we can't be left without some defence.'

'Make them serve,' one voice sounded from the back.

'We can't do that,' replied another. 'They're freemen, not slaves. And they have a right to be with their families.'

Alfred nodded. 'So I have a different idea. Let's say, as Wulf just said, we ask them to serve, but not all at once. Every man, thane or churl, will be required to serve six months out of a year in the fyrd and the other six months at home. Those who are serving should expect that those who remain will take care of their families and their farms in exchange for their safety. Then they will switch. And those who are serving will help build defence towers near the villages for people to run to in time of attack.'

Some discussion followed as the men talked about how to set up the new fyrd, and when the vote was taken, all agreed to the idea.

'Now,' said Alfred, 'we need to discuss a new set of laws. Our people have become very lax in the way they behave. With so much fighting, we have lost sight of how God wants us to treat one another. Some take whatever they want, even lives if they have murderous plans. Some people cheat others, thinking it is only good business, and still others slander and ruin reputations. We need to draw up a list of laws that people must keep and set punishments for those who break the laws.'

Here one of the bishops rose to speak. 'We can easily set up laws based on the Ten Commandments. That is the clearest way to do as God commands us.'

Some of the thanes looked a little uncomfortable, knowing they would have trouble keeping some of the commandments themselves, never mind making others obey them.

'How will we punish people? How will they understand what is fair?' Stiltherd, a broad-shouldered thane, wanted to know.

'We'll use the wergild system,' Alfred replied. 'Values will be assigned to everyone and thing. If a man steals a cow and butchers it, then he must pay the owner the wergild value. The same if a man kills another accidentally. Instead of his family beginning a feud with the murderer's family, just payment must be given. If the murder is deliberate, then he must die.'

74

'So we would have to set out what a person is worth, and his cows, land and everything else? What about if he slanders someone? What's the price of that?' someone wanted to know.

'His tongue hurt another, so cut it out,' replied someone else.

Alfred held up his hand to stop the growing debate. 'This is good. We need to talk about all these details and we need them to be written down. Brother Edric, as we decide each law, would you please record it. Then the monks can make copies to be sent out to every village and read to the people.'

For several weeks the Witan worked on the laws. Alfred encouraged them to make the punishments fit the crime so that everyone would understand why they were being punished. In the end the list was completed and sent out. Alfred prayed that his people would obey the laws and there would be peace and order in the land.

Over the course of several years, King Alfred and the Witan made many decisions that helped improve the kingdom of Wessex. They instituted fairs and markets for people to gather and sell their wares. The Saxons produced particularly good pottery and fine jewellery. Alfred suggested that they start building ships and training men for a navy in case enemies should attack from the sea. The Witan also decided what taxes the people should pay.

'Collecting the taxes will not be a popular job,' observed one of the thanes. 'The people will complain.'

Alfred had an answer ready. 'This is what you tell them. The king plans to use the money this way. One half of all the taxes will be used to fund the kingdom: to pay the fyrd and the fortifications, to pay the artisans who produce their wares, and to pay for a school to educate thanes' children. The other half will go to God: to care for the poor and sick, to rebuild the churches that were destroyed in the years of war and to found two new monasteries, one for men and another for women.'

The thanes agreed.

The Witan met many times to discuss and perfect the laws and organisation of village life. Meanwhile, Alfred still had something more he wanted to do, something for himself and something that would benefit his people.

One day Alfred came into the King's Hall and saw his twelve-year-old son Edward and Brother Edric. They sat side by side with a book between them. Brother Edric pointed to the words on the page and Edward sounded them out. Alfred stopped and listened, not wanting to disturb them. But Edward had heard the boots on the wooden floor and turned to see his father. With a big smile, Edward leapt up from his bench to greet Alfred.

'Father, do you want to listen to me read? Brother Edric has taught me lots of words.'

'Yes, I would like to see how you're coming along with your lessons. A prince must be as proficient with learning as he is with weapons. So, read for me,' he commanded with a smile.

Brother Edric had stood up respectfully when he saw the king, and now handed his pupil the heavy leather bound book, open at the page they had been studying. Edward stood straight with exaggerated importance and began to read the words slowly in Latin.

'I lift up my eyes to the hills. From where does my help come? My help comes from the Lord, who made heaven and earth.'[2]

Edward stopped and looked up, eager to hear his father's praise. Alfred did not disappoint him.

'Well done! You have applied yourself well. And you too, Brother Edric.' Alfred nodded in the monk's direction. 'How I wish I could have done this at your age,' he continued, taking the book from Edward's hands and holding it with reverence. He then fell silent as he leafed through the pages full of handwritten marks he couldn't understand.

'Why didn't you learn to read, father?' Edward asked. 'Didn't *your* father think it was important?'

---

[2] Psalm 121:1.

Alfred looked up and shook his head. 'That was not it at all. Come, let me tell you a little of my father and mother, so you will appreciate what you have now.'

Alfred moved to sit on the bench with Edward while Brother Edric bowed silently and left father and son to talk without being overheard.

'Your grandfather was a great warrior. He fought off many invaders and kept this kingdom safe. He was also a good Christian, and once Wessex was stable, he decided to make a pilgrimage to Rome to see the pope. He left the kingdom in the hands of my older brother and took me along with him.'

Edward looked surprised. 'You've been to Rome? What's it like? Was it as beautiful as they say?'

Alfred nodded, remembering the long journey and his father's joy at seeing St Peter's Basilica in Rome. 'The pope agreed to see us. I was only six years old, but he spoke to me and prayed for me, asking God to protect me and grow to be strong in my faith. I felt like that was a very important moment.'

'But why wouldn't your father let you read?' Edward wanted to know.

'It wasn't that he wouldn't let me. It was just that there was no time to teach me.' Edward still looked puzzled. 'Before we went to Rome, when my father was fighting so many enemies we could never stay in one place very long. We were always on the move, including all the women and children to keep us safe. And, of course, I had to learn to fight. Military training was more useful than book learning just then. Although, my mother did want me to learn, and all my brothers too.' Alfred smiled at the thought of his mother. 'She had a book of poetry she used to read to us. One day she offered the book to the first of us who could memorise the entire book. I went to work right away, and won the book before any of my brothers had hardly begun. I had hoped to keep that book safe, but...' he shook his head sadly.

'Was it lost?' Edward asked in a quiet voice.

Alfred nodded. 'When I returned from Rome, my mother had died and so had my oldest brother. My father died two years later and then I was expected to help my remaining brothers defend our kingdom. One by one they were killed in battle, so that I, a fifth son, became king. And no time for learning. Until now.' Alfred looked at the book he was still holding and then up at his son. 'It's time for me to learn too.'

'You?' Edward asked astounded. 'But you're the king.'

'But not too old or proud to learn,' Alfred said as he stood up. 'Brother Edric,' he called across to the hall. 'Come here, if you please. There's something I want to discuss with you.'

The monk rose from the table at the far end of the room and came immediately to stand before the king and await his orders.

'Brother Edric, you now have two pupils. I want to learn to read and I want you to teach me.'

The monk blinked in surprise but answered calmly, 'As you wish, my lord. When would you like to begin?'

'Now is a good time. And we'll see who learns faster, the father or the son.' Alfred gave Edward a playful punch to the shoulder.

Later that year Alfred called for Brother Edric to come to the King's Hall and bring his quill pens, ink and paper. Edric arrived, his monk's rough gown swishing against his legs as he hurried over to the table where the king sat. Bowing awkwardly with his arms full of his writing materials, he then took the seat that Alfred indicated across from him.

'I want to write some letters,' Alfred explained. 'I will dictate and you will write.'

'Yes, my lord. Who shall I address them too?'

'The best scholars.'

Brother Edric frowned. 'Who would they be?' he wanted to know.

Alfred shook his head sadly. 'We have none in Wessex. With the many years of war, our learning and literacy has all but disappeared. Besides you and a few other churchmen, and now Edward and I, who else can read and write? I want to summon the great men to come and teach us. So pick up your pen and let's invite the best to come: Asser at St David's Monastery in Wales; Bishop Werferth; Grimbald, the Flemish scholar; John, the Old Saxon and Plegmund, the hermit. I want to have these men here teaching us all how to read God's Word so that we may serve him better.'

So the letters were sent and over the next two years the scholars and churchmen came. Alfred welcomed them into his court. By this time Alfred had mastered the Latin language and had begun to learn English[3]. And what joy he felt when he was able to read from the Latin Bible.

'Listen to this, Grimbald,' Alfred said as he read aloud from the Psalms,

> 'The LORD is my strength and my shield; in him my heart trusts, and I am helped; my heart exults, and with my song I give thanks to him. The LORD is the strength of his people; he is the saving refuge of his anointed.'[4]

'My father used to quote those verses before he went into battle. I have remembered them from the time I was a little boy.' He paused, and seemed to come to a decision. 'Grimbald, I want you to teach me how to translate. I want to know how to choose the right words to express what the Psalms say in the language of my people. All my people should be able to read God's Word in their own tongue.'

Grimbald studied the king for a moment. 'It is difficult work, my lord, but certainly I will teach you. It will take a long time, but

---

[3] English: What we refer to today as Old English, used from about the fifth century to 1100.

[4] Psalm 28:7-8

if we ask John, the Old Saxon, to help us it would cut the work in half.'

Alfred smiled. 'Good! I can't wait to study God's Word. Meanwhile, I have another translation project in mind. Many of our priests have been ill taught how to minister to the people. Pope Gregory wrote an excellent book on how to be a pastor[5]. Could you and John see to the translation of that book into English? Then we can send it out to the priests for their instruction. And while we're at it,' Alfred's enthusiasm was building, 'I think we should translate the Ten Commandments in Exodus. Every Christian should know them and be able to read them too.'

Grimbald shook his head, but smiled. 'That's a lot of work, my lord, but certainly worthwhile.'

Alfred nodded and then opened his Latin Bible. 'So how do we begin?'

---

[5] Gregory's book was called *Cura Pastoralis* or *Pastoral Care*.

Who Are Those Guys with the Funny Names?

Names have changed over the centuries. What parents named their newborn son during the early middle ages was very different from today. But just because they were different, and sometimes hard to pronounce, doesn't make them any less real people. So how did they become famous scholars?

Asser was a Welsh monk from St. David's in southern Wales. We don't know when he was born, but we do know that he was sent to the monastery to be educated by a kinsman, Archbishop Asserius. He did so well as a student that he stayed on and became a monk so he could continue his studies and serve God. When Alfred invited him to his court, Asser wasn't sure he wanted to come. He liked the monastery and his studies in God's Word, but after a year, he agreed to come for half the year and spent the other half at St David's. He wrote a biography of King Alfred called the *Life of King Alfred*. He finished out his life as Bishop of Sherborne from the 890s until his death in 909.

Werferth spelt his name several different ways Werfrith, Waerfrith or even Hereferth. Why, we're not sure, but it could be that since Anglo-Saxon spelling rules were still not set yet, he was still experimenting with what looked best. The first time we read about him in history is when he was consecrated the Bishop of Worcester in 873. Later Alfred invited him to join his court to help with teaching and translation work. He died in 915 during the time of Alfred's son, Edward's, reign.

Grimbald, or Grimwald (again with the confused spelling), was born in what we call France today in 827. He joined a Benedictine monastery around 840 and was ordained a priest in 870. Grimbald became a well-known translator. King Alfred first met him when he broke his journey to Rome at Grimbald's monastery. Later when Alfred invited him to come to England, Alfred wanted to honour him by appointing him Archbishop of Canterbury. Grimbald agreed to come and help with the translation work, but preferred to remain a monk. He died shortly after Alfred himself in 901 at the age of seventy-four.

John, the Old Saxon, is a more elusive character, but at least he had a name we still recognise today. We do know he was probably born and grew up in the Frankish empire. After he was invited to England, Alfred appointed him Abbot of Athelney, a monastery that Alfred established in his previous hiding place. John recruited men from France as well as Saxon men to join the religious order. There is no record of where or when John, the Old Saxon, died.

Plegmund, or Plegemund (here we go again), was first known as a hermit who lived on an island at Plemstall in Chester. Hermits, living by themselves, have plenty of time for study as well as prayer. When monks visited him they discovered he was also a scholar. That's when Alfred heard of him. Plegmund had skills in both translation and administration, so after Grimbald turned down the position of Archbishop of Canterbury, Alfred appointed Plegmund. Plegmund reorganised the church, creating new parishes. He also improved the scholarship in the church and the translation work, replacing poor and incorrect translations of church writings. He lived long after King Alfred and crowned Alfred's son, Edward, and became his trusted advisor.

Who Turned out the Lights?
A.D. 900-1350

Alfred had to go to war again against the Danes in the last years of his reign so he was unable to finish his translation of the entire book of Psalms. But he had begun a project that many would later continue.

When Alfred died he left a stable kingdom for his son, Edward, to rule, and by the time his grandson, Athelstan, was crowned king in 925, most of England was united into one kingdom. However, the next two centuries saw repeated threats and raids until finally in 1066 the French invaded and stayed. William the Conqueror took the land and gave various parts of it to his loyal knights and they built castles and fortified towers. He changed the system of government and the language from English to French in the courts and houses of the nobility. The average person still spoke English, but the language of power became French, and those who were educated now had a new language to learn.

All over Europe boundaries continued to change as nations invaded other nations, vying for the best land. And with that came the same changes that happened in England; new people in control meant new leaders, new laws and often new languages. Keeping up with these changes was difficult for the average person, who had his family to feed and keep safe. On top of all this, terrible diseases called plagues began to spread. By the fourteenth century Europe was swept with the Black Death. It began in India and China and arrived in Europe via trading ships that carried diseased rats and their fleas. People were bitten by the fleas and with terrible swiftness they died a painful death within days. Medical knowledge was limited, so people didn't understand how the plague spread and they did all the wrong things to stop it. By 1348 one third of the population of Europe were wiped out by the plague and the next year one third of England's people had died.

Historians have sometimes labelled the years 476 to 1000 as the Dark Ages. That doesn't mean there was no light then, or that everyone suddenly became stupid or foolish. It simply meant that learning and bookmaking became less and less available. As a result there are fewer written accounts of life at that time than in any other period of history. And it's no wonder when people didn't know if they too would be the next to die, either from the plague or an invading army. The only places of learning left were the monasteries and the church.

The church too was having its problems. The popes were not always the kind of churchmen they should have been. Some became more interested in wealth and politics than properly running the church. Priests were not always trained as they should have been, especially because it became more and more difficult to obtain copies of the Scriptures. If the priest lived and worked near a monastery, he could go and read the Bible there. But those who served in more remote areas had difficulty making long journeys. Roads were few and bandits were many. Few people left the safety of their villages.

In the midst of all these changes God kept his Word safe. The monks continued their work of copying out the books of the Bible carefully by hand. And this was happening all over the western world. Then, when the times became somewhat more stable, God raised up scholars and theologians to take up the task of translating once more.

One such person was John Wycliffe. John was born around 1324 in Yorkshire[1]. Very little is known of his early life, but we do know he was very bright for he was sent to the new university in Oxford to study and then he remained there to teach. But John was not destined to have a quiet teacher's life, mainly because he also became a priest and insisted on preaching God's Word at some very inconvenient times. And then there was his new idea of translating the Bible for the common people.

The English nobility still spoke and read French, from the time that William the Conqueror arrived in England. They could afford to pay for French language Bibles to be sent from France. But the common people continued to speak English. Languages change over time; words change their meanings, new words are invented and some old ones discarded. The English translations made several hundred years before in King Alfred's time had changed dramatically. A new translation was needed, and God chose John Wycliffe to begin it.

---

[1] See map on page 229.

A Ray of Light

A.D. *1377-1384*

The crowds of people shifted restlessly in the side chapel of the London church. The Archbishop of Canterbury sat in his gilt chair and Bishop Courtenay stood by him scowling at Dr John Wycliffe seated before them. Wycliffe was dressed in the simple long dark tunic of a priest with his hooded cloak draped over his shoulders. His grey hair was partially covered by a black cap, while his long grey beard covered the upper part of his chest.

'Stand up!' Courtenay ordered. 'And answer the complaints we have against you.'

John moved to stand up, but then felt a strong hand on his shoulder pushing him back down into his seat.

'He stays seated,' the authoritative voice of the Duke of Lancaster announced behind him. 'The only complaint you have against this good man is that he tells you truths you don't want to hear. And I'm here to protect him.'

John sighed, wondering just how this was all going to turn out. The answer came sooner than he expected. Just as Bishop

Courtenay began again to read out his list a mob of people forced their way into the chapel.

'Have them removed!' the bishop shouted, but his command went unheard in the roar of the London mob.

'Where's the Duke of Lancaster?' someone in the mob shouted.

'Get him! He takes everything and leaves us with nothing!'

People began to push and fight. Furniture was overturned with a crash. Suddenly John felt a heavy hand wrap around his wrist, pulling him to his feet. It was the duke himself.

'This way, Wycliffe, out the side door. Be quick, man!'

Together priest and duke ran, ducking between and around brawling tradesmen and churchmen. As they emerged onto a side street, the duke shouted for his horses. A startled servant turned and saw the dishevelled pair. Realising his lord was in peril he ran down the street leading the horses. The duke, a seasoned soldier, swung up onto his mount with ease, but the servant had to assist John. Not used to riding, John had some trouble with tangled clothing as he tried to seat himself astride.

'Follow me,' the duke called and set out at a gallop down the narrow streets. John held on to the reins with determined effort as his horse followed close behind.

Not many minutes later they rode into the courtyard of the Savoy, the duke's home, and the gates banged shut behind them. The duke laughed as he slid gracefully from his mount. He turned to John with a smile of triumph showing through his neatly trimmed black beard.

'Well done! We outwitted them today!' and he held out his hand to help the priest down.

John dismounted less gracefully but landed on his feet before his powerful patron. He did not share the duke's view of the situation.

'The mob wanted to kill you,' John pointed out. 'They are as angry with you as the church leaders are with me.'

The duke shrugged. 'But they didn't succeed, now did they? Come, let's see what's for supper. I'm famished.'

John shook his head as he watched the duke head for the heavy door of his grand home, shouting for servants and giving orders. He appreciated the duke's kindness in rescuing him and for being his patron when many didn't want to know him, but he didn't think this partnership could last much longer. Their goals were too different.

John wished he were back at his beloved Oxford University, doing what he loved best, teaching theology to eager students. He had done so since he had graduated himself from Oxford over twenty years ago. Of course, it was that teaching that had gotten him in trouble. The more John had studied the Scriptures, the more he became convinced that the way some of the church leaders behaved was wrong. Some bishops, in England and in other countries, had amassed huge fortunes in both money and land. Their excuse for doing so was to fund the work of the church, but in fact these bishops lived like kings while the poor around them suffered from lack of food and work. John had also criticised the pope for telling people he was the final authority in both the church and the kingdoms. The pope had declared that kings should answer to him because he, the pope, was God's representative on earth. John taught his students that there were no such instructions in God's Word.

John sighed and stretched his sore limbs. The sudden violent ride had made his legs and back ache.

'Dr Wycliffe, would you follow me, if you please? My lord duke has called for you to join him in the hall,' the steward said. The man was about John's age, although well rounded from good food and easier living than most. John nodded and followed the man inside the large two-storey wooden house. The main corridor opened up into a large hall with several wooden tables set up lengthwise. They were empty at this time of day. But at the far end the duke sat at a table set on a raised dais. A servant was bringing in platters of cold meat, cheeses and bread, followed by another carrying a large pitcher of wine. As John walked the length of the hall he noticed the colourful tapestries hung on the walls for both decoration and to keep the drafts from outside to a minimum. Behind the dais hung the Lancaster's coat of arms which displayed lions for England, the fleur-de-les for France and castles for Castile and Leon symbolising his wife's home in Spain.

'Do stop gawking, man, and come and have something to eat,' the duke ordered affably. 'You are too much underfed.'

John smiled. 'I eat and drink what is necessary for the body,' he replied and took his seat beside the duke. With a nod he consented for the servant to pour the wine into a pewter cup and then served himself with a small portion of each item on the platters.

'There now,' the duke continued in between bites of meat. 'I think we can say we won today. Those clerics have no right to tell you or me what to do.'

John's hand and mouth froze, poised to take a bite of warm bread. Then he carefully set it back down on his plate and turned to his patron. 'My lord duke, I think you have misunderstood what I'm trying to say to the church. Don't forget that as well as a teacher, I'm also a priest. Of course, I must obey my leaders in the church. And, I want you to understand I don't think every priest or bishop is corrupt. Only some have misused their power as churchmen to enrich themselves. They are the ones who should repent. And, if I may beg your pardon, we are all, from the king to the lowest peasant, still answerable to God himself.'

'Yes, yes, of course I must obey God,' the duke replied. 'But I'm the son of the King of England. Why should a priest have the right to tell me how to help my father govern our country? And why should they steal all the good land and reap all the revenues from the harvests and the flocks and herds and then refuse to pay any taxes! They are the very ones who have the money to pay. We can't fight this war with France without weapons!'

John shook his head. 'We say the same things, but we mean them differently. I think the wealthy churchmen should give their money to the poor. Just look how broken and suffering the whole country is now. The Black Death has swept through the land twice in twenty years. Whole villages have died, whole counties are without leadership. Even the church has suffered because so many of the priests died with their people. Fields have not been planted. No one knows who owns which land because many families have no one left to inherit. The people are afraid and hungry. They need to be fed and given direction, from both the church and the king. That's why, if you will pardon me my lord, the London mob wanted to kill you. You just want to take the money away from the church to use for your own means.'

The duke stiffened and glared at John. 'I'm the king's son,' he repeated. 'I have a huge household to run, castles to take care of. People expect me to act like a prince of the realm. And then I need to have money for the war. These are things the people forget, and so do you, priest.'

John bowed his head and spoke softly. 'My lord duke, I do not wish to argue with you. I think I need to go back to Oxford and do what I do best, teach. And you too must do your job, but if you please, take care that you remember you must serve God even though you are a prince.'

The duke rose abruptly from the table and left the hall without a word. John pushed his plate of food from him, no longer hungry. He looked up to see the servants standing rigidly by, unsure what to do.

'I think I will leave now,' he said to them. 'Would you mind packing up the food on my plate for me to take on my journey?'

Relieved to have something to do, the young men quickly cleared the table. As John was putting on his cloak, one of them returned with the food wrapped up in a cloth.

'May God speed your way, sir,' he said.

John nodded his thanks and left the duke's home. It was a long journey on foot from London to Oxford, but John was used to walking wherever he went. And he welcomed the quiet time to pray as he walked. He prayed for the duke and the king that they might rule the country well, for his students that they might be ready to hear and understand God's Word, and for the people in his parish church that God would comfort them in their distress.

Back in Oxford, John settled into his usual routine: lecturing to his students, continuing his own studies and preaching to his congregation in Ludgershall, Buckinghamshire. But it didn't last long. The following year he was summoned once again to London, this time to answer charges of heresy from both the archbishop and Pope Gregory. His students urged him not to go, fearing that he would be unfairly tried and convicted, but John just shook his head. 'I must obey,' he replied. 'Besides, what better opportunity will I have to present God's truth?'

So back he went with a few friends. As he had the year before, they passed through many lifeless villages falling in to ruin now that all the inhabitants were dead from the plague. But this year John noticed more fences than before. Some men were taking advantage of all the empty places to claim them as their own. They enclosed the land to keep others from taking up the same idea. And they met groups of landless people looking for work. These people could have threatened them, but they respected a priest enough to leave him alone. England was not a happy place.

Once more John stood before the Archbishop of Canterbury sitting in his gilt chair and Bishop Courtenay, Wycliffe's enemy and accuser. And once more charges were read out followed by a disturbance. There was no mob this time, just a royal messenger who rushed into the middle of the proceedings. He made his apologies with a respectful bow and handed a sealed letter to the archbishop. Amid the quiet mutterings of the spectators, the archbishop broke the seal and read the letter silently. John stood patiently waiting to hear the outcome. Passing the letter to Bishop Courtenay, the archbishop shook his head. Bishop Courtenay's eyes widened with surprise which quickly turned to anger.

'It seems you have yet another patron, Wycliffe. How do you manage it?' he asked sarcastically. Waving the paper at him, he continued, 'Princess Joan appears to like what you preach. She says that we can pass whatever judgements we want here, but she will use her power to prevent them from being carried out.' Courtenay threw the paper down in disgust. He turned to the archbishop.

'My lord, will you allow this to happen?'

The archbishop shrugged. 'There is nothing I can do about it. We will have to let him go. But I will say this, Dr Wycliffe,' he said turning to face John. 'Remember you're a priest of the church and you must follow its teaching as taught by the bishops and the pope.'

John stood tall and replied, 'I follow the teaching of God as found in his Word, the Bible. This I have always striven to do and to teach.'

At that moment John felt a tremor beneath his feet. He looked down and then noticed the wooden rail in front of him shift. Looking around he saw others with panicked expressions on their faces. All around them seemed to be shifting and shaking.

'Get out!' Courtenay bellowed. 'It's an earthquake!'

John gathered up his cloak and quickly followed the crowd of people pushing for the door. By the time they were all standing outside, the shaking had stopped. No one had been injured, but there was general confusion amid the relief. This seemed like a good time for John to slip away. As he made his way out of the city he was grateful that God had sent yet another person to shield him from the wrath of Bishop Courtenay. He would write the Princess a letter of thanks once he was safely back in Oxford.

John found his students waiting for him and the news of what had happened in London. There was great relief all around when they heard of the last minute letter. But John didn't dwell on how close he had come to prison. Instead, during his travels he had had time to think. He thought of all those people who were now without priests in what was left of their villages. They couldn't

afford to pay a priest's salary, but they still needed to be ministered to. So John called all of his students together to hear his idea.

'Remember in Mark's Gospel how Jesus sent out his disciples in twos to preach to the people? I would like to send you out to do the same thing. I want you to go out to the villages where they have no priest or church anymore. I want you to preach Christ to them. Tell them the good news of the gospel. Comfort them in their troubles and lead them to the One who loves them. Will you go?' he asked looking around at their young faces.

The response was unanimous. 'Tell us where we should go and we will gladly share the gospel with the people.' And so the preparations began. Soon the young men, taking only a few possessions with them, went out two by two to the villages preaching and teaching about Jesus. The people received them well, but certain bishops were not happy. These men had not been properly ordained or sanctioned by the church. Who were they to teach the common people? But the bishops knew they couldn't touch Wycliffe without angering some of the royal family.

John ignored the complaints and criticisms, mainly because he was becoming occupied with another idea. If the people were to understand the way of salvation then they needed to be able to read God's Word. But the people spoke English and most of the Bibles were still written in Latin or French. He called together his close Oxford colleagues and told them his plan.

'The Latin language Bible we use now is the same translation that Jerome made all those centuries ago in Palestine. He did an excellent job, but now the only people who speak Latin are churchmen. Latin is not a holy language, just an old one. King Alfred translated the Psalms and Bishop Dunstan before him, but it was in Anglo-Saxon English and no one understands that anymore. We need a complete and accurate translation in the English[1] the people speak today. So I propose to start a translation project to translate the New Testament. Will you help me?'

John Purvey agreed at once. 'It's just what we need to properly teach people from God's Word. And I think we should use some of our students, the ones gifted with languages to help us. It will sharpen their skills and train the next generation to take over from us.'

---

[1] The English language referred to here is now known as Middle English, used from about 1100 to 1500.

Nicholas Hereford nodded. 'Very good idea. Let's set up a room with all the materials we need so we can work together, helping each other with the difficult passages.'

John was pleased at their enthusiasm, but felt it was only fair to point out the major problem with their project. 'You do realise that you are risking your careers here at Oxford. The archbishop will be angry with us for going ahead with this translation without his approval. And I imagine Bishop Courtenay will accuse us of vulgarising the Word of God by making it available to unlearned peasants. In one way I understand his concern about people misusing God's Word, but God doesn't need bishops to protect himself or the Bible. So let us pray for wisdom as we translate and protection from persecution.'

Over the next four years the scholars and students worked diligently to translate the New Testament from the Latin Vulgate version of the Bible to the present day English. They each took a book to work on, but they also took time to read each other's work and discuss the best words to use to convey the meanings. John was most concerned too that they make no mistakes, so the translations were checked many times. By 1382 the New Testament was completed.

In that same year the archbishop died and Bishop Courtenay became Archbishop of Canterbury. One of his first plans was to have Dr John Wycliffe removed from his position at Oxford. John met with the Chancellor of Oxford in his study.

'I'm sorry, Dr Wycliffe, but I have no choice,' Chancellor Rygge explained. 'Both the archbishop and the king have ordered me to remove you, Nicholas Hereford, and your other colleagues. I tried pleading with them in my last visit to London, but I didn't succeed. You must leave Oxford.'

John nodded, not at all surprised. 'I'm an old man,' he replied. 'I will go to my parish in Lutterworth and preach to my congregation and write. That will be enough for me. The others will not be stopped just because they can't teach here anymore. We will all preach God's truth wherever we are as long as God gives us breath to do. John Purvey will carry on the translation work for me. I am content.'

Where Did Universities Come From?

The word University comes from the Latin phrase *universitas magistrorum et scholarium*, which roughly means 'community of teachers and scholars.' Just like the monasteries were communities of monks, so the universities gathered together students and their teachers. In fact, the university system grew out of those monasteries.

If you were a bright young man (sorry, no women allowed) during the early middle ages, then you would have been sent to a monastery to be taught and trained as either a monk or a priest. Everyone assumed that all scholars should be in the church since that was where all the learning took place. However, if you were a promising young student around the time of Alfred the Great's grandson, Athelstan, then you might have a choice. Your father could still send you to the monastery, but if he didn't want you to become a monk he could choose to send you to a 'freelance' teacher in a nearby town. These teachers, who had been trained in the monasteries, received permission to teach and set up shop on their own. There would have been no campus with lecture halls or residences. You would probably rent a room in your teacher's home or in a house nearby. Everyone in the town would know you were a student by the 'gown' you wore. The gown was similar to the monk's habit or cloak, and generally black. In medieval times everyone had a place to be and a job to do, and you were identified by what you wore.

Then several things began to happen. Some exceptional teachers began to attract students from different countries in Europe. So if you were a student in Oxford around the twelfth century you would have met students from France or Italy or

99

maybe Germany. Each student brought with them new ideas and ways of doing things. You would also have new subjects to study. Today we have all sorts of subjects to study in school and think nothing of it. Between the time of King Althestan and John Wycliffe new subjects like science and medicine, as well as non-Christian literature, were introduced. The universities were drifting away from their church roots, so they decided to become a more separate organisation. They chose a spot to build or bought buildings for permanent lecture halls. Not wishing to be left out of the universities altogether, some of the monasteries decided to build student residences or dormitories where they could supervise students and their behaviour. The king got involved too, issuing a charter and appointing a chancellor who was responsible for the university. If you were a fellow student of John Wycliffe, you would have had a choice of several colleges or residences to live in such as Merton College. Or you might have even been a student at Balliol when Dr Wycliffe was the master teacher. These were exciting and changing times!

The Stirrings of the Reformation
A.D. 1350-1500

John Wycliffe only lived two more years, dying of a stroke in December 1384. John Purvey carried on with the translation of the New Testament. He revised it so it read more smoothly, using more words that the common person was familiar with. A few years later Nicholas Hereford began translating the Old Testament. Many of Wycliffe's students continued to go out into the countryside to preach and were known as the 'Poor Priests or Preachers.' Not everyone approved of their efforts and called them another name: Lollards. It was a term of derision from the Dutch word that means to mutter or mumble. When a violent revolt began among the peasants, the Lollards were blamed for stirring up the people. But in fact the people were incensed by a new poll tax that they could not afford to pay. The uprising was put down easily by the king's army, but the Poor Preachers were persecuted from then on.

Meanwhile, life began to settle down in Europe. Countries became more stable, many with hereditary monarchies that brought some order to the society. Not all problems ceased, of course. Wars flared up between countries every so often over who owned what city or countryside. Civil unrest happened when no one could agree who should inherit a throne. And the threat of contagious diseases was always close at hand. But life in the later Middle Ages was less chaotic than it had been a century or two before. As a result the arts began to flourish. It started in Italy around the time of Wycliffe and spread throughout Europe over the next three centuries. People gifted in painting, sculpting, music and science began creating what we now know as famous works of art and inventions. This time period was called the Renaissance, a word that roughly means 'rebirth.' People now had time and relative safety to use their creative talents.

God is, of course, the source of all creativity, and he gave creative gifts to many people at that time. To one man in particular, Johan Gutenberg, God gave the ability to invent new things. Johan was born in what we call Germany today and he was intrigued with how things worked. Not only that, but he kept asking himself the question, *What if? What if I try this? Would it work better if I take this part and move it here? What if I add these two parts and remove this one?* He experimented with machinery until he finally came up with an invention in 1434 that would change the world. He invented moveable type.

Moveable type, you ask? So what? Well, moveable type was used in the first printing press ever built. At first that might not sound too exciting or even important. But remember how books had been produced until this time? People, mainly monks in monasteries, carefully copied out by hand each book, taking a long time. Naturally, there were not many copies of each book to be had because they took so long to produce. And only the rich could afford to pay for them. But Johan's invention meant books could be printed rather than handwritten much more quickly and cheaply. God had planned for this invention to be available just as he was causing other events to occur in Europe.

The church too was going through changes, and not all for the better. Some popes had gathered more power and land for their personal use. They especially wanted all the European kings to ask the pope's approval for their policy decisions and to pay taxes to the papacy. The kings didn't like the idea, but when they refused they discovered how powerful the pope had become. When King Ferdinand of Naples, an Italian state, fell out with Pope Innocent VIII in 1489 over Ferdinand's refusal to pay taxes to the pope, Innocent excommunicated Ferdinand. Excommunication was the worst form of punishment at that time. There were two parts to the punishment. The first was spiritual. The pope declared that the person was no longer a Christian and had no hope of heaven. Secondly, an excommunicated person was cut off from everyone. No one was allowed to speak to them or have anything to do with them, and anyone was free to kill the excommunicated person without fear of punishment. That was a dangerous place to be, especially if you were a king because the pope could take your kingdom away from you. And that is just what Pope Innocent VIII tried to do. He offered Naples to the King of France and that provoked a war between the Italian states and France.

While the great men argued, the common man was left to live his daily life as best he could. Everyone considered himself a Christian then. There were many who didn't really believe but they were careful not to say so too loudly or they would be excommunicated too. So everyone went to church, did their best to listen to the priest and obeyed whenever the pope issued a command, called a bull. But there were also people who truly believed. They worshipped with sincerity, desiring to serve God and obey his commands. It was from this group of Christians that God raised up some very influential men who were about to change things. The men themselves didn't plan to cause all the changes that took place. They were just concerned with obeying

God's Word. But when obedience to God clashed with obeying the pope or king, then suddenly they had choices to make. Who would they serve? Would they have the courage to remain true to God?

In 1506 Pope Julius II decided on a costly building project. He wanted to rebuild the great church of St Peter's in Rome. However, there wasn't enough money in the church treasury for the project, so he came up with an idea. It was actually an old idea thought up by another pope, Boniface IX, at the end of the 1300s. The plan was to send priests around the countryside selling indulgences. What is an indulgence? The word 'indulge' means to be given something pleasurable that you don't really deserve. We often use it today to mean someone who has enjoyed too much of something, like ice cream or chocolate. What it meant in the medieval church was freedom from punishment. When people went to the priest to confess their sins, the priest would give them punishment or penances to perform to show their repentance; things like saying so many prayers a day or fasting for a certain period of time. If the priest gave you an indulgence, then you were freed from having to perform the penance. So Pope Julius II, and the popes who came after him, thought if the people paid for those indulgences then he could use the money to build the church. Since all people sin and are supposed to confess their sins, he was assured of raising lots of money and the people would be happy not to have to perform any penance. But not everyone agreed that this was a good idea, especially those who read their Bibles, where nothing was said about performing penances or purchasing forgiveness from a priest or a pope. But not enough people had Bibles in their own languages. More translations were needed so people would know the truth. And God had chosen just the men for the job.

A Disturber in the Church
A.D. 1516-1522

Clutching his leather bound copy of Paul's Epistle to the Romans, Martin Luther climbed wearily up the stone steps of the church tower. At the top he didn't pause to look at the view, but sank down onto the wooden bench, the only piece of furniture in the small room. How tired he felt, like an old man instead of a young professor of Holy Scripture at Wittenberg University.[1] Even his spirit felt sore. He hoped up here, no one would bother him and he'd have time to read and pray.

The book of Romans fell open on his lap at the section he would be lecturing on the next morning, but Martin didn't take up his reading of the hand-copied words right away. He sat with his head resting back on the stone wall, his eyes closed. Since coming to lecture at the university four years ago he had not stopped working. It seemed that every time he turned around, someone gave him a new job to do. First, he had been elected sub-prior at the monastery where he lived, which meant he had daily preaching

---

[1] See map on page 230.

duties and Scripture reading duties at evening meals. He was forever, it seemed, being asked to preach at the city church, often by the Duke of Saxony himself. He had to supervise the studies of his students and those novices studying to become monks. Then he was elected vicar of eleven monasteries in the area making him responsible for their pastoral care. He had been appointed a court representative for the people in Herzburg if they were called to appear in court at Torgau. He lectured at the university every week day morning at six and then at one in the afternoon. He was writing a commentary on the book of Psalms and finally somehow had ended up being caretaker of the town's fishpond. Martin would have laughed if he had the energy. But none of those things were the real problem.

Martin had happily accepted most of those responsibilities and on the good days he enjoyed carrying them out. But on the bad days, it was a different story. Today was a bad day. Martin felt as if the darkness in his soul had leaked out and sat heavily around his shoulders like an inky cloud. He woke up at morning with the same fear that had plagued him the night before. He prayed desperately, confessing his sins and pleading for forgiveness but he had no peace. Instead, he worried he had forgotten to confess a sin, or maybe God, who could see his heart, knew he wasn't really as sorry as he should be. These same thoughts and fears had bothered him for years, however hard he tried to stop sinning and do what was right and good. He had tried to be faithful in obeying God and serving him. Look how busy he had been these last four years doing the Lord's work!

Opening his eyes he looked down at the book in his lap. He had been lecturing to his students on the righteousness and justice of God. It was all there right in the first part of Romans. If God was so just how could he, Martin, expect God to overlook his sinful heart? 'Serve God,' he had been told over and over by his teachers in the monastery and he tried with every ounce of his strength. But all he got for his efforts were fearful nights, black moods and an overwhelming sense of being lost. *O God, help me*, he prayed.

As Martin began to read from the beginning again, the familiar words began to take on new meaning. When he came to the phrase 'The righteous shall live by faith,' he stopped. Faith, not works, was emphasised here. Not what *he* did, but what *God* gave him, faith to believe in Jesus Christ. Martin continued reading with eagerness, his weariness suddenly forgotten. He read the entire book of Romans seeing God's wonderful offer of salvation to an undeserving people. Not only was God just, but he was also wonderfully loving and merciful.

With a growing understanding, Martin closed the book and quickly walked down the tower steps already thinking about

what he would say in his lecture for tomorrow. How much he had to tell his students, and those who would come to the church tomorrow, and in the monasteries, and anyone else who would listen. Martin chuckled. Maybe that's why he had ended up with so many things to do. He could tell so many people about God's Word.

The following year Martin was still busy with all his duties of preaching, teaching and writing when a rumour reached him about a Dominican friar called Johann Tetzel. Some of Martin's congregation at the Wittenberg church came to tell him what they had seen in the town of Juterborg.

'It was a great parade, led by one of the town's officials carrying a long pole with a cross and the papal crest on it. Father Tetzel came next carrying a gold cushion with documents on it,' one man informed him.

'Yes,' another chimed in. 'All the officials were there dressed in their finest and they were the first ones to put their coins in the box and get a paper.'

'Paper?' Martin asked. 'What is Father Tetzel selling?'

'Indulgences,' a young woman said. 'I bought one for myself, and one for my grandmother. My sins are taken care of, and my granny is now freed from purgatory. I wish I had more money to buy some for all my family who have died.'

'What!' Martin shouted. The group of people took a step or two back as they saw the anger on his face. 'You can't buy salvation or free anyone from purgatory!'

The young woman was startled and then began to weep. 'You mean I haven't helped her? Is she still suffering? I thought I was doing the right thing.'

Martin patted her shoulder awkwardly. 'I know you thought so,' he said more gently. 'You were misled by Tetzel. He should know better.'

Martin was angry that Tetzel was lying to the people and giving them false comfort. Martin excused himself and went to his study. When angry like this he needed to write. He would write out everything he thought was wrong with what Tetzel was doing. How awful that Tetzel was doing it for the pope! How could the head of the church tell people that they could purchase salvation for themselves or their relatives? He knew this idea was not new. Six years ago he had been in Rome where he had been troubled to see priests and monks selling indulgences. Now that he understood that salvation was a free gift from God, he was angry that the very churchmen who should know God's Word, were teaching the people wrong doctrine just to raise money to build churches.

Martin was worried too. He didn't want his students or the people of Wittenberg to be fooled into thinking Tetzel was right. When he finished writing out how and why Father Tetzel and Pope Leo were teaching against what the Bible said, he took the 95 theses and nailed it to the church door. This door was the town's bulletin board. Everyone who could read would see that Tetzel was wrong. Martin also sent a copy of his theses to Archbishop Albrecht, who had also supported Tetzel's campaign to sell indulgences. He wrote a letter too and pleaded with the archbishop to examine these practices and compare them with God's Word. He also warned him of the grave danger of God's anger for misleading his people.

Martin was not surprised when the archbishop sent his letter and document on to Pope Leo. He was concerned, though, when he received a summons to appear in the city of Augsburg the following year to explain his actions and the 'new' doctrine he was preaching. He asked his friend and vicar-general of the Augustine order of monks, Johann von Staupitz, to go with him. Von Staupitz agreed and brought along some lawyers too.

When they arrived in Augsburg, Luther and von Staupitz entered the newly built mansion of Jakob Fugger, banker to the pope and European Heads of State. The mansion was enormous with a gleaming copper roof. Martin felt dwarfed by the large rooms and splendid furnishings, all so different from his own lodgings at the monastery attached to St. Anne's church. Martin was nervous, not because he had changed his mind on the indulgences question, but because the man he was about to face had great power. Cardinal Cajetan had been commissioned by the pope to examine Martin's beliefs and have him recant any that were not in line with the church's doctrine. Martin was glad von Staupitz and the lawyers were with him. He hoped they would help him if he got into difficulty. Then Martin shook his head. He was already in difficulty. All he could hope for was that it wouldn't get any worse.

They were shown into a smaller room with carved wooden chairs set up in a row before a table. A fire burned cheerfully in the ornate fireplace behind the table taking the chill off the October air. Martin and his party sat down. Another door opened a minute later and Cardinal Cajetan entered dressed in red robes and cardinal's hat. He was followed closely by a younger churchman carrying pen, ink and paper, who would record what was said at the meeting. He settled himself at the table while the cardinal stood by the fireplace studying Martin. Martin swallowed and stood up respectfully. He was the youngest man in the room.

'Your Grace,' Martin began. 'I have come as you commanded.'

'So I see,' the older man replied dryly. 'And have you come to recant your beliefs as outlined in the treatise you posted or have you continued to preach and teach?'

Martin remained silent.

The cardinal fixed his eye on Martin and said, 'You are a disturber of the church. Have you forgotten the vows you took as a monk and a priest? You promised to be obedient to your superiors, which includes me and the pope. He has given his blessing to Father Tetzel for the work he is doing for the church.

You have no right to raise questions or debate this matter. It has been decided.'

Martin stiffened and returned the cardinal's glare. 'So, teaching the truth is the same as disturbing the church?' Martin shouted. 'Which is more important, the truth or the peace of the church?'

Von Staupitz reached over and pulled on Martin's dark monk's tunic. 'Softly,' his friend and teacher advised.

'I'm not here to debate with you, Father Martin. The pope speaks with God's authority. If you dispute that, then you are in error. Think on that,' Cardinal Cajetan said leaning forward and placing his hands on the table that stood between him and Martin. 'Then come back tomorrow and tell me you recant.' The cardinal turned abruptly and went out the door he came in without waiting for any reply. The clerk hastily gathered up his writing materials and followed his master out of the room.

Shaken, Martin turned to his friend and the lawyers who were rising from their seats. 'Why will he not debate?' Martin asked the group. 'Surely we should be able to discuss these matters to arrive at the truth. Is the papacy so closed-minded?'

'Come,' said von Staupitz. 'We need to discuss our strategy further. You must at least sound reasonable, Martin, and not lose your temper. Maybe tomorrow he'll be willing to listen.'

But the next day went no better. The cardinal insisted that Martin was disobeying the pope and therefore God. Martin replied that he couldn't deny the truth of God just to please a man, be he pope or not. Truth mattered more than peace. The cardinal dismissed Martin again, telling him he had one more day to recant.

As they walked back to the monastery that evening, Martin said to von Staupitz, 'What should I do? I don't want to disobey my superiors when I have taken vows not to do so. Can the cardinal be right? Are my vows more important? Am I taking too much on myself to challenge them?'

'If that is what's worrying you, then why don't I release you from those vows? I have the authority as vicar-general of the order to do so. Then as you pursue this matter, no one can accuse you of breaking your vows.' Von Staupitz put a hand on Martin's arm. 'My son,' he finished softly. 'You must do what is right in God's eyes, not man's.'

One of the lawyers came hurrying up behind them. 'Father Martin, I just heard that there is a good chance you'll be arrested tomorrow when we go to the mansion. Maybe it would be a good idea to slip out of town tonight before anyone realises you're gone.'

No one said a word. Instead, all three men quickened their pace to the monastery where Martin packed up his few belongings and then knelt in front of Johann. Von Staupitz spoke aloud the formal words for the lawyers to hear, releasing Martin from his monastic vows. Then he urged Martin to go with one of the lawyers who would help him leave Augsburg unnoticed. Meanwhile, von Staupitz would stay and inform the cardinal late tomorrow that Martin had gone.

Once they both returned to Wittenberg Martin and von Staupitz went back to work. Von Staupitz reported to the Duke of Saxony what had happened and the threat that the cardinal had issue against Martin. The duke shrugged.

'Luther is *my* professor at *my* university,' the duke replied. He settled his large body comfortably in a beautifully carved oak chair. 'Pope Leo will think twice before doing anything to Luther. After all, the pope needs my vote for the next emperor.' The duke smiled with satisfaction. 'Tell Luther to carry on teaching and preaching as he has been. Someone has to speak the truth and I will protect him so long as he continues to do so.'

When Martin heard of the duke's protection he praised God and continued to speak out against the wrong practices of the church. But he was careful to tell his students and congregation that they must still come to church, pray and read God's Word. It was only certain churchmen who were in error, not the entire church.

A year later another summons was issued, but this time from a fellow theologian at the University of Ingolstadt, Dr Johann Eck. Eck wanted to debate with Martin in public, hoping to show that Martin was wrong and putting an end to the controversy. Martin accepted. This was the very chance he wanted, hoping that the wrongs in the church would be made public and corrected at last.

A huge group of people set out from Wittenberg to go to Leipzig for the debate. Martin asked another friend and fellow professor, Philip Melanchthon, to go with him. Together they travelled the forty miles in a horse-drawn wagon, followed by 200 of their students armed with axes and sticks to protect their professors. An equal number of students and supporters of Eck greeted them as they arrived in the city of Leipzig, along with a large body of guards hoping to prevent any violence. The debate went on for eighteen days with both men arguing carefully and thoroughly each doctrinal point. Luther, a gifted speaker, spoke with clarity and humour. Eck, equally gifted, spoke with great seriousness and craftiness. By the end, Eck had manoeuvred Martin into admitting that if he challenged the idea of indulgences, then he was challenging the pope himself. If that was so, then Martin was questioning whether the pope was really God's representative on earth, as the church had taught. If the pope was not, then Martin was saying the entire church was in error for listening to a man who was not speaking for God.

Martin and his party returned to Wittenberg feeling defeated. He had failed to convince Eck about the error of indulgences and instead had come close to being labelled a heretic. He was thankful he had a safe place in Wittenberg, under the care of the Duke of Saxony, but he wondered how the duke could keep him safe if the pope decided to excommunicate Martin. Time suddenly seemed very short.

Martin decided that the church leaders and people should know what God's Word said about these subjects. He wrote many small books in the German language and had them printed on the new Gutenberg printing presses and delivered to cities all over the German states. He carefully outlined what the Bible taught about faith and salvation, the role of church leaders, and how Christians ought to worship and live. He denounced the pope himself, saying he had no place in the church or politics. He rejected the church's teaching on elements of the Mass and he advocated marriage for priests. These revolutionary books caused uproar throughout Europe and Martin received a summons once more, but this time to be tried before the new Emperor Charles V.

Martin began his journey to the city of Worms, where the trial was to be held, with fear and worry. Would he be condemned and killed? But as his journey in a wooden cart progressed through the countryside, crowds of people gathered. They shouted encouragement to Martin and clapped as he went through the small towns. Some joined in the procession following the cart part of the way. By the time Martin had reached the city of Worms he was full of hope that God would protect him. But those feelings deserted him the very next day.

Imperial guards marched Martin into the Bishop's Palace through the crowds of spectators. His heart began to beat faster when he saw the young emperor on his throne with the dukes of the German states seated on either side of him. The only friendly face among them was his protector, the Duke of Saxony. Could this one man protect Martin from the rest? Sweat began to form droplets on his forehead. His legs felt unsteady as he was forced to stand while, von Eck, his appointed prosecutor, advanced into the room, bowed to the emperor and dukes and then turned to face Martin.

'Are these your books?' Eck demanded, pointing to the table set up in the centre of the room.

Martin took a few steps closer to the table piled with books and pamphlets and replied, 'Yes.'

'Do you renounce them?' Eck shouted.

Fear suddenly paralysed Martin. He couldn't speak. All around the room the spectators fell silent and the dukes began to lean forward, waiting to hear the answer. After a few minutes Martin finally managed, 'May I have time to think and pray before I answer?'

The prosecutor snorted in disgust, but turned to the emperor for a ruling. The young emperor hesitated. He was still getting used to his new position, and he was more concerned with the political consequences of this trial than the religious ones. Finally he nodded and said, 'We will meet again tomorrow. Then we must have your answer.'

The emperor rose and left the room with the dukes. The prosecutor ordered the guards to take Martin back to his lodgings and the crowds respectfully made way for the professor in monk's clothing.

The night was long for Martin. He prayed and paced and prayed some more. His answer would determine the rest of his life. If he recanted everything he had written, saying he was wrong, then he would be forgiven by the pope and allowed to continue teaching and preaching. But he would only be able to teach what they wanted him to teach. Martin would be safe but he would have to deny the truths taught in the Bible. If he refused to renounce the books then he would most likely be arrested, excommunicated and executed. A fearful choice. There was only one right answer and Martin prayed the whole night through that God would give him the courage to say it.

The next day Martin stood once more in the presence of the emperor and dukes. Once more the prosecutor demanded that he recant his works. Martin took a deep breath and replied.

'My books fall into three categories. The first has been approved by the pope some time ago and I will not renounce what we all agree is true. The second category includes books where I denounce the church's wrong teachings. I have not changed my mind on those, so I will not renounce them. The third group are pamphlets I wrote against certain church leaders who are deliberately misleading the people. They are wolves in sheep's clothing. I admit my language is harsh and unkind, but I still believe them to be correct. I will not renounce these either. May God help me.'

The emperor rose to his feet in anger. 'Take him away. I will pronounce judgement later.' And he swept out of the room.

All around Martin the spectators murmured, some angry, some pleased. As Martin marched down the city street again, crowds gathered along the roadside cheering him. It lifted his heart from the depths of the fear he had been feeling.

A few days later Martin still had not been called back into the emperor's presence, but someone else came to visit him instead. Duke Philip of Hesse arrived with news that Martin had permission to travel safely to say goodbye to friends and family before the emperor pronounced judgement. Martin was amazed but didn't question the opportunity. He quickly gathered together his few belongings, and with a few friends slipped out of the city to the waiting cart and guards.

Martin travelled for a week, meeting people and preaching in various places. Then one evening Martin noticed the guards he had been given dropped away leaving him and his two companions to go through a wooded area alone. The sun was getting low on the horizon when suddenly a group of horsemen appeared. One of them rode over to the cart, pushed one of Martin's friends aside and grabbed him by the back of his tunic. Martin was lifted up still clutching his knapsack and flung over the horse in front of the rider. Off they rode as Martin bounced painfully on the neck of the galloping horse.

After a time the horsemen slowed down and allowed Martin to sit upright on a spare horse they had with them. Then they stopped at a small hut in the woods where Martin was told to remove his monk's habit and put on the clothing of a knight.

'But why?' Martin asked. 'What's going on?'

'You have been abducted,' the leader said with a smile. 'We're taking you to Wartburg Castle where you will be safely hidden while the great men debate your fate. The Duke of Saxony has it all arranged.'

Martin sighed with relief. God had provided a way of escape for him. He would be safe, even though he had defied the pope and the emperor to remain true to God's Word.

Martin lived at Wartburg Castle for a year, with most of his friends thinking he was dead. He grew a beard and longer hair and he was given the name Knight George. Everyone assumed the poor knight was a distant relative of the duke. Only the castellan knew the truth. He had rooms prepared for Martin and books brought so that Martin could use the time to continue his studies and writing. And the most important task he took up was translating the New Testament into German. Martin wanted the German people to be able to read God's Word for themselves and be able to understand it. The Bibles that were being printed now were still in Latin, which most people in the German states could no longer read.

Martin worked diligently, checking and re-checking the original Greek and Hebrew for the clues to the exact right word in German that should be used. It was just the right time to be doing this. Few people knew Martin was alive, so no one came to visit. He had no distractions or duties beyond his translation work. In just over a year, Martin completed the translation. At the same time it became safer to travel back to Wittenberg, where the Duke of Saxony offered him safe haven. Martin returned, rejoicing.

As soon as his German New Testament was printed, it sold 500 copies in the first two months and it continued to sell steadily for the next decade. But Martin didn't stop there. Next he planned to translate the Old Testament into German. And he wanted to meet some of the other reformers in Europe that he was beginning to hear about. One of them was a young Englishman by the name of William Tyndale.

Libraries and Illuminated Manuscripts:

If you have a shelf of books in your bedroom, or anywhere else in the house, then you own a library. A library is simply a collection of books, although today many of our public libraries also contain collections of DVDs, books on CD, maps and other items that you can borrow. Libraries have existed since people have been writing and making books, all the way back to ancient times. One of the most famous libraries in ancient Egypt was in Alexandria, which at one time had collected over 400,000 books. Actually they were rolls of parchment since the book or codex was not being used yet. It must have taken a small army of librarians to keep that library tidy!

Romans, too, had large libraries, both privately owned and publically available. So when the Roman Empire collapsed after the Vandal tribes sacked Rome, monasteries seemed the safest places to gather up and store the many books and parchments. Later, when monks got into the bookmaking business, the monastery libraries grew even larger. No wonder the monastery became the place for students to learn with all those books so handy for research.

The monks made books to earn money as well as to preserve learning. They needed to pay the expenses of housing, feeding and clothing all those who lived in the monastery. So they often took private contracts to make books for wealthy people. These people didn't want just a nicely handwritten book. They wanted a work of art, something that would look nice on display when they weren't reading it. So monks with artistic talent began to illuminate the books. Illumination is not really a picture, although that could be part of it. The monk would use gold or coloured inks to decorate the printed text. For example, if the first words on the page were 'Our Father,' as in the Lord's Prayer, the first letter 'O' would be drawn much larger with the coloured inks, and designs would be drawn within the letter. It would also be outlined and decorated with the gold ink. This was done throughout the manuscript, usually the first letter on the page or chapter. The front covers were often decorated too with coloured pictures and Christian symbols along with costly jewels glued on. It made for a beautiful, and heavy book when it was all done

To be fair, this was not just a moneymaking business. It was also considered a way of expressing love and honour to God, especially when they were illuminating his Word. One of the most famous illuminated manuscripts from the early days is the Lindisfarne Gospels that is now in the British Museum.

Translator on the Run

A.D. 1524-1526

'Dr Luther, I'm so pleased to meet you,' William Tyndale said in German as he entered Martin Luther's study. Martin, still wearing his monk's habit even though he was no longer a monk, looked up from his piles of open books and manuscript paper. He laid down his pen and stood up to greet William.

William felt somewhat awed to be standing in front of such a famous man, although he was not quite what William had expected. Martin was a sturdy man, well filled out in face and body, not particularly attractive yet he was vibrant and full of life. William shook hands and felt the strong grip of the forty-year-old man. William, by contrast, was ten years younger with a leaner build and a long face. He had also endured much less persecution and difficulty in his life than this famous man. But there was one thing William knew he had in common with Martin Luther: the conviction that the Bible must be translated into the common language in every country.

'What brings an Englishman to Wittenberg?' Martin inquired while waving a hand toward an empty upholstered chair by the small stone fireplace.

'I had to leave England because of threats to my life,' William explained as he sat down. 'I tried but failed to get permission from the Bishop of London to begin a new translation of the Scriptures. When I began the work anyway, it became too dangerous to stay. It's against the law in England to make unauthorised translations. A friend in Hamburg suggested that I should come to the university here to study the German language. I would like very much to be able to read your books and study your translation of the New Testament.'

'You speak German very well.' Martin said. 'Do you really need to study the language?'

'Oh, yes,' William replied, leaning forward, his enthusiasm for his subject growing. 'Translation is such an intricate business. It is much more than just a matter of finding a good word in one language to fit a word in another language. Each language has a special sound or cadence, and then there are the idioms: those phrases that are so clear in one language, but when literally translated make no sense in another. So I need to study German more closely to understand better.'

Martin smiled. 'It's good to meet a scholar so thirsty for knowledge.'

William returned the smile and leaned back in his chair. 'Would you mind if I asked you some questions about your translation work? I want to speak with someone who has worked on it much more than I have.' Then, not waiting for Luther's reply, William plunged in with his questions and thoughts. 'It seems to me that it is better to translate from the Greek New Testament rather than the Latin. The Greek word order in the sentences is the same as both English and German. What about you? Which version did you use? Jerome's Vulgate is very good, but I think the new Greek translation by Erasmus is better. And I was having another thought. What about dividing the books into chapters, making it easier to find passages? I know it's never been done before, but I think it would be helpful.'

The men spent that afternoon and many after it discussing the finer points of translation. They met in between Martin's many duties and William's continued studies. William admired Martin's work and made many notes about Martin's translation of the New Testament.

After several months William finished his studies at Wittenberg University, but continued to work on his translation of the New Testament. He was also searching for an amanuensis to help with the work. It wasn't until he had almost finished that he finally found one.

As William was leaving Wittenberg University one afternoon, a slim, energetic monk rushed up to greet him. He was dressed in the long black cloak and white tunic of a Dominican friar.

'Dr Tyndale,' he said, grasping William by the hand and shaking it with determination. 'I hear you're in need of an assistant. I've just arrived here from England, having had to flee for righteousness' sake. How humbled I am to be suffering for the gospel, much as you and other reformers are!'

William pulled back in surprise and looked the man up and down. He was neither young nor old, but he did have a nervous energy about him. 'You have studied translation work?' William asked doubtfully.

'Oh yes,' the monk assured him. 'I did a great deal of work at the monastery in Greenwich. My name is William Roye.'

William hesitated. He wasn't sure he and this man would get on, but his promised helper, a friend from England, had not arrived and William needed someone now to help get the manuscript ready for printing. 'Let's see how we get on together,' William finally said. 'But first I want to leave Wittenberg and go to Cologne. There are many more printers in that city, so I should be able to find one who will print my translation for me. Are you willing to go with me?'

Roye nodded vigorously. 'An excellent choice. The city is right on the River Rhine with access to many places in Europe. I'll pack my belongings right away.'

William nodded, still feeling reluctant about his new companion.

They left the next day, stopping first in Hamburg to pick up a little money a friend had left for William, and then went to Cologne. William planned to come into the busy city quietly and rent a room in the poorer part of town so as to be unnoticed. Roye was less pleased with the idea, hoping for a little more comfort. However, William had more important uses for his money.

After settling into their lodgings, William set Roye to work copying out parts of his translation that needed a clean copy. Sometimes when translating, William had chosen a word or phrase, and then had second thoughts, stroked it out and added a different one. He couldn't give those to a printer to use. While Roye copied in his best handwriting, William went looking for a printer.

The August sun beat down on William as he walked the busy narrow streets. People were going in and out of the many shops or stopping at the open air booths to buy everything from food to clothing and books. As he neared the great cathedral he stopped to admire the work still under construction. In the last two hundred years the enormous eastern part of the grey stone church had been finished but, the tower, higher than William had seen in any city, still had several stories to go. A wooden crane sat on top, but no workmen were working today. Turning away, William headed for the streets known for the printing business. Spying the one he wanted, he entered the shop, stooping a little to get through the low doorway.

Inside, William stopped to survey the work of the print shop. On the right a young apprentice was leaning over one of the many tubs of water. Neat piles of metal trays and clean linen rags surrounded him, all to be used to make paper. Straight ahead was the printing press, a large wooden apparatus fashioned from enormous wooden beams with a wooden bench attached to it. Two men, one with his back to William, were busy feeding the press. The older man had a small roller covered with ink. He rolled it on the rectangular metal plate that sat in a tray. Another young apprentice laid a large sheet of paper on top of the plate and slid the plate and paper under a second metal plate hanging above. The older man lowered the upper plate by turning a large wheel. As the top plate pressed down on the paper and lower plate, additional weight was added. A few moments later the weight and upper plate were released and the paper carefully slid out and lifted off. The apprentice carried the paper by the corners to the left side of the shop where lines, strung across the area, held other sheets of drying paper. As he pinned it in place, he noticed William and he cleared his throat loudly. The older man turned around.

'Good day to you, sir,' he said as he put down the roller and wiped his hands on his large brown apron. 'May I be of help to you?'

'I hope so, Master Quentell. I have a printing job for you.' William responded.

'That's what we do here. Would you like to see our work?' Quentell led William toward the washing lines of drying paper. 'See here,' he said, pointing to the closest large page. 'We print quartos, four pages at once. When the ink is dry the pages can be folded, cut, and bound into the books, with all the other completed pages.'

'Very impressive,' William said as he looked carefully at the font and spacing. 'How long does it take?'

'Depends on the size of your book. What takes the most time is laying out the plates with the letters,' Quentell replied, leading

William over to the printing press where he could see that the large rectangular plate was really a tray that held tiny metal letters. 'We can only do four pages at a time, but we print as many copies as you want, or can afford,' he added with a smile, 'and then we move on to the next four pages.'

'I have money to pay,' William assured the printer. 'I'd like 3,000 copies printed.'

Quentell lifted his grey bushy eyebrows in surprise. 'And what may I ask will I be printing so many copies of?'

'An English translation of the New Testament,' William replied, watching the printer's face intently.

The older man wrinkled his brow and stroked his clean shaven chin. 'That's dangerous work you are asking of me.' Quentell studied William's face for several minutes. William waited, hardly breathing. Finally, the printer said, 'If I do this I will need extra payment. We should be compensated for breaking the law.'

William sighed. He told Quentell how much he had and the printer agreed to start, but William would need to find other financing to finish the print run. William had a few ideas, thinking of the various English merchants living in the city who might be willing to help if they were sympathetic to the Reformed cause.

All went well at first. Roye worked on the clean handwritten copies and then took them to the printing shop. William visited a number of merchants that worshipped with the small Reformed congregation in the city and found enough money to complete his project. But then, catastrophe struck.

One day Roye entered the print shop, arms full of paper. 'Here's the rest of the book of Matthew,' he announced in a loud voice.

Peter Quentell's head snapped up from the tray of type he was arranging and he glared at Roye. 'Have a care, man!' he replied in low tones. 'I'm expecting another client at any time. No one must know what we are doing.'

Roye was annoyed by the public correction, especially when he noticed the two apprentices by the water tubs laughing at him quietly. 'I know *that*, but this work will change the whole of England once it's published. It's difficult to keep silent about such a thing.'

'Keep silent about what?' a new voice asked from the doorway. All of them turned to see a man in his forties dressed in a black broadcloth cloak with a fur collar and a soft felt hat set on greying hair.

Peter Quentell went to greet the newcomer with a smile. 'Dr Cochlaeus, welcome to my shop. Please come this way and we'll discuss the book you want published. Here, let me show you how the press works.'

As Cochlaeus walked toward the printing press, Quentell stepped behind him and with his hands motioned to one of the apprentices to take the papers from Roye and put them away in a cupboard. As the apprentice moved to obey, Quentell joined his new customer at the press and began a detailed description of the process. As they turned to look at some of the finished pages hanging on the lines, Quentell noticed Roye still stood in the shop. He glared at him, hoping he would take the hint and leave. However, Cochlaeus also saw him and remembered his question.

'What are you keeping silent about?' he asked again, this time looking closely at Roye.

'Oh, you know authors,' Quentell began, interrupting Roye as he was beginning an explanation. 'They will go on about how important their writings are. I'm rather tired of hearing him boast and told him to keep silent. He naturally objected,' Quentell finished with a smile. 'My apprentice will give you the pages we finished yesterday, Master Roye. Then you can come back in a day or two to collect some more.'

Still annoyed, but aware that he should not dispute with the printer in front of strangers, Roye left the shop. He decided not to tell William about what had happened in case he had to listen to another lecture on being discreet.

Several days later, Roye returned to the print shop to find Cochlaeus seated at a table checking over some printed pages. Roye stood uncertainly in the shop door until Quentell noticed him and motioned him to a point furthest from Cochlaeus.

'More pages, Master Roye,' Quentell said in a normal voice. 'Karl,' he called over to one of the apprentices. 'Please bring Master Roye's finished pages.'

Roye looked about anxiously, wondering why Quentell was not being more secretive.

'Don't worry,' Quentell said quietly. 'We need to make this business appear as normal as possible.'

Karl arrived at Roye's side with a few printed sheets. He looked dreadful, as if he had been out drinking the night before. 'This is all we have,' he mumbled.

Quentell frowned at him but said to Roye, 'We have to go slowly, printing when we can safely do so.'

Roye nodded and turned to leave. As he passed Cochlaeus, the man looked up and studied him intensely. Roye, suddenly nervous, rushed out the door and into the street.

The next evening William and Roye were walking back to their lodgings when Peter Quentell's young grandson came running down the lane, papers clutched in his hands.

'Dr Tyndale, you must fly from here! My grandfather's shop is being raided by soldiers and they're seizing your print run. I was sent to warn you that they'll come for you next.' The boy panted in between the words. He thrust the papers at Roye. 'These were all grandfather could save for you.'

William wasted no time. Taking the papers, he called 'Thank your grandfather for me,' as he started to run toward their rented room. 'Roye, where are you? Come on, man. Do you want to be arrested?' he called back to his assistant still rooted to the spot. Suddenly Roye came to life and began to run after William, catching him up and reaching their room first. When William rushed in the door, Roye was hopping about excitedly but unable to decide what to do. In exasperation William pushed him toward the table strewn with papers and books. 'Pick them up!' he ordered. 'We have to take as much with us as we can and get out of the city before they close the gates for the night.' Roye obeyed, and together they scooped up their belongings, threw them into bags and rushed out into the street. 'This way,' William directed. 'Its a quieter route and it will be less likely that we'll be discovered.' I know a way to the city gates.'

Full dark was just settling on the countryside when William and Roye stopped to rest. Setting down their bundles under a tree, they both sat down looking back at the city they had just escaped from. They were far enough away not to be seen by any vigilant guards, with a good view of the road in case anyone should come upon them.

'All that work,' Roye moaned. 'Now it's all lost, and the money too.'

William nodded glumly. Quentell's grandson had managed to save the first twenty-two chapters of Matthew, but the rest of the printed work was gone. Fortunately, he still had some of his uncorrected pages that Roye had copied from, but even so he would have to start the project all over again. Another unpleasant thought occurred to him. He turned to Roye.

'I heard you boasting to the apprentices one day that this translation would make you famous. Did you tell anyone else?'

'Of course not!' Roye was indignant, but William saw fear in his eyes.

'What about when you went to the tavern last week? Did you have too much to drink and forget to be silent?'

'It wasn't me,' Roye insisted, 'but it could have been those apprentices. Maybe someone tricked them.' Then warming to the idea, Roye told William about Cochlaeus' interest and how awful Karl, the apprentice had looked one morning.

William cut him off. 'Stop chattering. It doesn't matter now. I need to think.' Roye fell silent but fidgeted with his hands, twisting and wringing them. William stood up suddenly. 'We'll go to the city of Worms. That's where Dr Luther defended his theses. The city supports his teachings, so we should be safer there.'

Roye leapt to his feet and began gathering up the bundles. 'The further away from Cologne the better,' he said, and started out on the road to Worms.

When they arrived a few days later they found lodgings in a poorer neighbourhood. And once more William went in search of a printer while Roye set to work copying out again a clean copy for the printer. William chose Peter Schoeffer, the leading printer in the city.

'Master Schoeffer, it is good of you to take on my project and to be willing to do it so quickly. But I've had an idea that might make the job even faster and a little cheaper for me. Instead of printing the New Testament quarto sheets of paper, could you print on octavo sheets instead?' At the printer's puzzled look, William went on to explain. 'I would like a smaller book, pocket-sized to literally fit into a pocket or up an open sleeve. It would make the books easier to smuggle into England and easier for people to keep them hidden when not reading them.'

Understanding dawned on Schoeffer's face. 'I print eight pages at once on the same size paper I was using for the quarto. Yes, that's an excellent idea. So now we need to calculate how much paper we will need so I can order it. I don't make my own, but there's a paper mill not far from here that makes very fine paper.'

Together William and Master Schoeffer discussed all the details of the transaction until both were pleased with the bargain. William gave Schoeffer a partial payment with a promise of the rest after he had spoken with some English merchants by the riverside.

Schoeffer for his part promised to stop all other printing jobs and have all his presses working on William's New Testament. The plan was to finish in six months.

William found the support that he needed among the English merchants, not only for money but also for an idea about how to smuggle the illegal Bibles into England.

'The harvest was very bad this year at home,' one of the prosperous merchants told William. They were sitting in a tavern having dinner. 'Cardinal Wosley has foolishly passed a law that says no one can take grain from one county to another to prevent people from hoarding food. But that means the cities are starving because they depend on the farms outside the cities to sell to them.'

William shook his head and his spoon paused over the stew he was eating. 'The Mayor of London must be furious.'

The merchant smiled. 'Exactly. And that's why he has contracted me to buy up as much grain as I can and ship it to the city.' He took a large swig from his tankard of small ale.

'That's good. At least the people won't starve,' William replied.

'Yes, yes, but it's good for you too. Don't you see? All those sacks of grain, many more than usual, will be shipped into the biggest city in England. So why can't each of those sacks also contain a few books, like your pocket-sized New Testaments?' The merchant sat back with a satisfied smile.

William grinned. 'Of course they can, my friend. As soon as the print run is finished I'll bring them to you. I'll even help you load them into the sacks.' Both men raised their tankards and took a celebratory drink.

By February, six months after they had fled from Cologne, William watched his Bibles being loaded onto ships sitting in the harbour. They would sail down the Rhine, out into the North Sea and then across to England. He praised God for bringing all the right people and opportunities together to cause it to happen. He now prayed that as many people as possible would find them and read them or listen to God's Word read in their own language.

William didn't stop his work. He now wanted to translate the Old Testament into English, and the city of Worms seemed as good a place as any to begin. There was a Jewish community in the city with some Hebrew scholars among them. William planned to consult with them as he worked from the original Hebrew language. But before that he had one change to make.

William returned from the riverside to their rented room. 'Roye,' William called. 'I want to speak to you.'

Roye rolled over in his bed where he had been when William had left earlier. He sat up and stretched. William surveyed him with disgust. He had never really trusted Roye since they had run from Cologne and now Roye was getting lazy too.

'Now that the Bibles are on their way, I think we should part company. I thank you for your help. I will pay your share of the rent and food until the end of the week and then you must be gone.'

Roye struggled out of bed. 'But what about the Old Testament translation? Don't you need my help with that?'

William shook his head. 'That won't be necessary. Let's not argue. Just make plans to leave as soon as possible. I'm sure a man of your ability will find work somewhere else.'

William left, feeling relieved that he was at last free from his annoying, and perhaps even dangerous, companion. William knew that once his Bibles were discovered by either the king's men or the Bishop of London he would be a hunted man. He would have to be very careful from now on about where he lived, who knew him and most importantly know who his enemies were. It would mean a life of sacrifice and hiding. He couldn't have many friends or they might suffer because they knew him. He couldn't afford to be seen too often or people might inform on him for money or other rewards. Those thoughts saddened him. But what brought joy to his heart was this: God's Word would be read by thousands of people, copies of the New Testament passed around from family to family, and people's minds and hearts would be changed by hearing and reading the gospel.

How Paper Was Made:

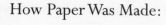

Paper was first invented in China around A.D. 100, but they were not about to share the idea. They kept the process a secret for 700 years. When Muslims invaded the eastern part of the Chinese empire and captured some Chinese prisoners, someone revealed the instructions. Soon the details of the invention spread throughout the Muslim and European countries.

In the fifteenth century old rags were first used to make paper. Recycling happened back then too! The cotton or linen cloth was soaked in tubs of water until they turned to pulp. This could take several days. Then the pulp was gently squeezed out and the fibres separated, and put once more into water (fresh water). A mesh screen mounted in a wooden frame was used to gently scoop out the fibres, shaken carefully to form an even surface, and the water drained out. This thin, damp sheet was laid out on a piece of felt. The process was repeated, adding several thin sheets on top of each other. The next step was to place a second piece of felt on top and press, squeezing out the remaining water and forcing the layers to become one. After carefully removing the felt on both sides, the paper was allowed to air dry. Just imagine how long that process took to make enough pages for a whole book. It would have kept an apprentice busy all day, every work day.

After a short time, it became apparent that there were not enough rags in Europe to make all the paper that was needed. So then the idea of going back to plants was suggested. But they had to use something that wouldn't run out quickly, like the papyrus had in ancient times? Looking at the heavy forests, the inventors decided to try trees. And sure enough, soft wood trees like spruce had excellent fibres that make good pulp that could be turned into paper. The same process was used, but as the centuries have moved on, large machines were invented to do the work of that poor over-worked apprentice at many times the speed.

What Happened Next?

A.D. 1526-1553

William Tyndale spent the next ten years running from King Henry VIII's and the Bishop of London's spies. William had broken the law by publishing a translation that had not been approved by the church. He had also offended King Henry with a preface that he wrote in later editions that criticised Henry's divorce from Queen Catherine and marriage to Anne Boleyn.

Because he was so good at hiding, historians cannot accurately say where William lived and worked during that time. All that is known is that he moved often, sometimes just ahead of soldiers who had come to arrest him, and probably lived in most cities in northern Europe for a short time. William continued his translation work of the Old Testament, although some of it was lost in a shipwreck that he managed to survive. In 1534 he settled in Antwerp in the home of an English merchant who was able to protect him as long as William stayed with him. William was finally betrayed by a young man posing as a friend but who was really working for the Bishop of London. William was arrested and sentenced to death in 1536. He was strangled and then burned at the stake. Before he died he was allowed to make a brief prayer. He spoke loudly for all to hear:

'Lord, open the King of England's eyes!'

God answered that prayer three years later in 1539. King Henry reversed the laws that were supposed to prevent people from reading the English Bible. Now he gave orders that every parish church should have a copy of another English translation of the Bible and it should be read out to the congregations as well as be available to anyone who came into the church to read it. This translation was known as the Coverdale Bible, named after Myles Coverdale who translated it. He used Tyndale's translation of the New Testament and the Old Testament books from Genesis to Deuteronomy, that Tyndale had managed to complete before his death. Then Coverdale finished translating the rest of the Old Testament from Jerome's Latin Vulgate Bible. The Coverdale Bible or Great Bible, as it was sometimes called, was the first complete English Bible to be published. It was also the Bible used in the Book of Common Prayer when it was compiled in 1549 under the direction of Archbishop Thomas Cranmer.

Tyndale, Luther and Coverdale were not the only reformers busy with translation work. Many men with language skills were also translating God's Word into every major European language. And there were more English versions too. William Whittingham was born in 1524 in Chester, the same year Luther and Tyndale met in Wittenberg. He was a brilliant young man, graduating from Brasnose College and All Soul's College. Then he travelled to France and Germany, attending a number of European universities. He was also briefly an ambassador for King Edward VI, Henry VIII's son, in the French court. But when William returned to England after his studies, he found life in his home country was about to become very difficult for Protestants.

An Englishman Abroad
1553-1560 A.D.

William Whittingham rushed along London Bridge, dodging knots of people as they were hurrying on their way home to avoid the threatening rain. Twenty-nine year old William wished he was going home too instead of trying to get out of London before the gates were shut for the night. He reached up to clutch his felt-lined beaver hat as a gust of wind threatened to take it off his head.

'Whittingham!' William heard a familiar voice addressing him with surprise.

He looked over the heads of some young women and saw a family friend he hadn't seen in quiet a while. He stopped and allowed the older man, clutching his long cloak against the wind, to make his way through the crowd toward him.

'Mr Harding,' William greeted him. 'How is your family?'

'Well, thank you. Your father told me you were at some university in France or Germany. When did you return?'

'A month or so ago. Just in time to hear the terrible news that King Edward[1] had died and the Protestant cause with him. I greatly

---

[1] Edward VI was the only son of Henry VIII. He died at the age of sixteen, after reigning for six years.

fear that his sister, Mary,[2] will make England unbearable for me with her strong Roman Catholic beliefs.' William shook his head with dismay. 'So now I must leave again.'

'Where to?' Mr Harding asked.

'Somewhere beyond the seas,' William replied dramatically. 'But I must get out of the city first. Then to Dover in time to board a ship leaving for France tonight.'

'May God go with you, William. I will tell your family I have seen you and all is well with you.'

'Thank you, Mr Harding. And may God protect you and yours from this popish queen.'

Without further delay William turned and continued to make his way to the other side of the bridge. Between some of the houses built on the stone bridge, William caught sight of the River Thames below rushing past in swirling eddies. Once he was across he turned to look back at the city one more time. Only God knew if he would ever be able to return to his homeland.

Later that evening he arrived at an inn in Dover. He knew a group of Protestants had arranged passage on a ship for any who could get there in time. He found the group at dinner, eating a sombre meal of fish, bread and cheese, served by a surly innkeeper.

'Are you another one of those?' the beefy man demanded when William entered the common room. When William nodded, the innkeeper jerked his head toward the table full of men and women and a couple of children. 'Go, have your last meal,' he said with an unpleasant laugh. 'I'm reporting you all to the authorities when you're done.'

'Why?' William wanted to know.

'Because a law has just been passed by our new queen that says no one may leave the country without first being interviewed by

---

[2] Mary I was Henry VIII's oldest daughter. She became known as Bloody Mary because of her persecution of Protestant Christians.

the local magistrate. And you lot haven't done that. I don't want to be in trouble for not reporting you when I know you're leaving on that ship out there in the harbour.'

William looked over to the group of men and women, waiting to hear from their leader what they should do. But no one spoke. They just sat and studied their plates, looking defeated. So William made up his mind to take charge.

'Innkeeper, bring some more food and small ale, if you please,' he ordered and sat down on a stool set at the end of the table. He introduced himself and learned the names of the fellow travellers by the time the innkeeper returned with the food.

As the innkeeper set the platter down in front of William, the door opened and several men entered. They called out orders for ale and sat down at another table. One of them, not too steady on his feet, tripped over a large greyhound sleeping on the floor by the table. 'Stupid dog!' he muttered.

The innkeeper came over and kicked the dog as it got up slowly and stretched. It yelped and hastily moved out of range. 'Out of the way, beast. You're upsetting my customers, just as much as our new queen is, but at least you're better to look at.'

The men joined the innkeeper in laughter. William paused in his eating, a thought suddenly occurring to him. Then he said to the group of people around the table. 'Eat up. We need to be away to the ship very soon.'

'But what about the innkeeper and the magistrate?' one young man asked.

William smiled. 'You leave that to me.'

After they had eaten their fill, they rose to leave.

'Not so fast,' the innkeeper called out.

'Don't worry,' William replied. 'I'll pay for the food,' he said, handing the man more than enough to cover the expense.

The innkeeper took the money and stuffed it in the pocket of his once white apron. 'Now, down to the magistrate with you,' he said.

'Well, if that's what you really want us to do,' William replied. 'I'm sure the magistrate will question us closely about what we've been doing today. I'll have to tell him I was at your inn, where I heard you insult the Queen, saying your dog was better looking that she is. Are you sure you want me to do that?' he asked quietly.

The innkeeper's broad face began to turn pale with fear. 'No, no,' he sputtered. 'It was just a jest. I meant nothing by it.'

'Ah, but would the magistrate see it that way?'

The innkeeper hesitated and shrugged. 'Makes no difference to me if you stay or go.' Then he deliberately turned his back to the group and William signalled them to leave quickly.

When they arrived at the ship, the captain refused to let them board, demanding extra payment for taking on illegal passengers. As William reached for the money in his small leather purse fastened to his belt, he breathed a brief prayer of thanks to God for his wealthy and generous family.

They arrived in France the next morning after a rough, windy crossing. William had somehow become their leader and marshalled the sorry-looking group of refugees to an inn he knew of in the town. Over the next few months William learned of other Protestant refugees in other towns and cities. He and his companions joined up with them and by the following spring the group of two hundred English Protestants had decided to move to Frankfurt, a free city in the midst of the German states. The Frankfurt city magistrates had already allowed a French-speaking Protestant congregation to use one of the city's church buildings.

The large group packed up their few belongings and began the journey across the northern part of France and into the German states. The roads were in poor shape and the men often had to climb out of the carriages and wagons to push the large wooden wheels out of mud or deep ruts. By the time they arrived in the German city, they were tired and hungry. They disembarked in the large town square and stood gazing around them. The square was surrounded by three and four-storey houses built with several types of stone used to make decorative patterns on each storey. The roofs were sharply peaked and sported numerous chimneys. The square itself had a large well for public use and many open air stalls that were full of goods for sale with eager shoppers crowded around them. Aromas of strange foods and the guttural sounds of the German language filled the air. The group moved closer together, feeling like the strangers and foreigners they were.

William looked around anxiously, wondering if the letter he had sent ahead of them had reached Valérand Poullain, the leader of the French-speaking congregation. He stopped an older man dressed in a bishop's long cloak and three-cornered black hat.

'Can you tell me how to find the Church of the White Ladies?' he asked in German.

'It's not far from here,' the bishop responded, looking at the crowd of travel-weary people behind him. 'You've had a long journey,' he observed. He then gave William the directions he needed and went on his way.

William suggested that the men find accommodation for their families while he went in search of the church and Monsieur Poullain. After a few wrong turns he arrived at the church door, and heard the words of Psalm 95 being sung in French. He waited just inside the church for the service to end and then introduced himself.

'Welcome,' Monsieur Poullain greeted him heartily. 'Come, I will introduce you right now to Johann van Glauburg, a member of the city council. He has been most helpful and sympathetic to our cause.'

William followed the cheerful Frenchman, who kept up a running commentary on the city, the people and anything else that came to mind. They left the building and walked a few short blocks to the city hall, an impressively decorated stone building. Here, in one of the ornate meeting rooms, William met the councilman. Glauburg was a prosperous man, wearing a short full gown of red brocade fabric overtop a doublet with puffed sleeves and short breeches of yellow and black. William bowed respectfully and Glauburg motioned for the two men to take a seat.

'Welcome to Frankfurt, Herr Whittingham,' the councilman began. 'Poullain told me of your coming. I'm willing to let you share the church building with his congregation, but I don't want any controversy. You must be willing to follow the same order of worship that the French Protestants use.'

William nodded. 'We can do that. All we want to do is worship God simply with singing, prayer and the reading and preaching of God's Word.'

'Yes, yes,' van Glauberg nodded. 'I understand that. But I don't want any of your people causing problems in the city or the emperor may regret we are a free city and decide to compel us to become part of his empire. So we all behave ourselves quietly here and hope the great man keeps busy with other matters. Do you understand?'

William nodded. He didn't want any trouble either and would encourage the English Protestants to behave as good guests in this foreign city.

Not long after everyone was settled in their new accommodations, the congregation met to elect a pastor. Since there were no ordained men in the congregation, William suggested they write to three clergymen who were also exiled from England and living in other European cities. Everyone agreed and William wrote the letters. Only one man replied that he would come. His name was John Knox.

Knox arrived several months later, reluctantly leaving his studies behind in the city of Geneva to minister to the congregation. At first all went well. The congregation appreciated Knox's preaching and passion for God. They also benefited from his wise council and pastoral advice. William and several other men were elected as elders by the congregation. They assisted Knox in drawing up a simple order of worship, similar to the French one and leaving out many of the elements of the Anglican liturgy found in the Book of Common Prayer. This was voted on and approved by the congregation.

However, during the winter more Protestant refugees from England arrived in the city, bringing with them a different opinion about worship. Led by Bishop Richard Cox, they wanted to use the Book of Common Prayer that they had used in England. They wanted the type of service they were familiar with and not something new, and they planned to deliberately disrupt the worship services until they got their way. So when one of the elders began the service, this group of people would call out the words from the Prayer Book. They ignored requests to stop and kept up the disturbing noise.

John Knox tried various ways to bring peace to the congregation. He tried to reason with the newcomers. Even William tried to explain that they had an agreement with the town council to remain quiet and well behaved. Then Knox tried preaching, telling the people that it was better to worship God in simplicity and that parts of the prayer book were wrong. Finally, William went to Councilman van Glauburg to warn him that serious trouble was brewing and to ask for his help. The councilman attended a meeting of the congregation and warned them all to behave or he would refuse to allow them to meet in the church building. Surprisingly the troublemakers agreed to do as the councilman had ordered, but that was only because they had another plan.

Bishop Cox sent two men to see other members of the council and gave them a copy of a pamphlet that Knox had written two years before.

'See here,' said one of the men as he laid open the pamphlet on the table before the councillors. 'Right here, Knox says that Emperor Charles[3] is worse than Nero, that terrible Roman tyrant who burned the city of Rome. What if the emperor should read this? He would be very angry. By allowing Knox to live in your city the emperor will think that you agree with what Knox has written. You must get rid of that man quickly before Emperor Charles decides to take vengeance against you.'

The councillors were shocked. After calling together their fellow councillors, they decided the best way to bring peace to the English congregation was to send Knox away immediately. Then it was the congregation's turn to be shocked. Most of them didn't want their pastor to leave, but van Glauburg told them they would either lose their pastor or their building. John Knox decided it for them.

'I will go,' he told the people sadly. 'I can continue my studies in Geneva. You have other men you can call to be your minister, men who are godly and caring.'

'I'm going with you,' William announced. 'I don't want to stay in a congregation like this. I'd rather go to Geneva too and study with John Calvin.'

Several other men spoke up and said they would go also. So the next morning the small group set out on foot to travel from Frankfurt to Geneva. The journey through the Swiss Alps was both difficult and beautiful. The mountains rose high, with narrow, rocky pathways around steep cliffs and slippery glaciers. Then the paths would open up into beautiful meadows full of spring flowers or deep icy blue lakes and rivers. But the sight that cheered the men the most after many weeks of travel was the city of Geneva sitting at the far end of Lake Geneva surrounded by mountains peaks.

---

[3] Emperor Charles V ruled over the Holy Roman Empire at the time. The Holy Roman Empire included what we today call Germany, Austria, Switzerland, Belgium, and the Netherlands.

As they entered the bustling city, John Knox led them to John Calvin's house where they were welcomed by his housekeeper.

'Monsieur Calvin is not here just now,' the older woman explained as she ushered them into a sitting room full of bookcases and books piled on furniture. She sighed and moved books off the chairs to allow the men to sit down. 'I will bring you some refreshment, while you wait. He shouldn't be long.'

As they were enjoying some spiced wine and honey cakes, Calvin arrived home and greeted Knox with a wide smile on his long narrow bearded face. 'My friend, how glad I am to see you, but I do grieve about the circumstances. How sad when Christians disagree with each other. But, now introduce me to your friends.'

'This is William Whittingham, John Bodley, Christopher Goodman, Anthony Gilby, and William Kethe. All fine men and loyal friends.'

William shook Calvin's hand with energy. 'I'm so pleased to meet you. I would like to study here with you if you will permit me?'

'A scholar, are you?' Calvin said with a smile. 'We always have room for those. Which languages do you know?'

'English, German, French, Latin, Hebrew and Greek.'

'With those languages you could easily be a translator,' Calvin said thoughtfully.

'Well,' William hesitated and then plunged onward. 'I have been trying my hand at translating some of the New Testament from the Greek. Possibly you might have a look at it and tell me what you think?'

'Indeed, I will. When did you have time to do this?'

'It's something I do whenever a moment allows. But coming here, I thought I could devote myself to the translation full time.'

'Monsieur Knox,' Calvin said turning to his friend. 'I think you have brought us a valuable man.'

Calvin assisted William and the others to find places to live and introduced them to the other Protestant refugees in the city, some of which spoke English and some Italian. William would have been happy to go to the French-speaking church that Calvin pastored, but Knox persuaded him to come to the English-speaking one.

'It is a small congregation, less than a hundred,' Knox explained, 'and many of them don't speak French. It would encourage them to have as many come out to the worship services as possible.'

William agreed and accompanied Knox and his friends to the Notre-Dame-la-Neuve, a lecture hall that Calvin used for his students, as well as a meeting place for the English and Italian Protestants. Each group took turns using the narrow grey stone building with its high small arched windows and massive double wooden doors. Once inside, William pulled his cloak around him for warmth. The thick stone walls kept the church cooler than outside. He made his way down the centre aisle and sat on a bench near the front. He looked around him appreciating the simplicity of the building with its arched ceiling and wooden beams. Then his eyes met those of a young woman sitting across the aisle. From her white cap her dark hair hung down in ripples around her shoulders and back, signifying her unmarried state. She was modestly dressed in a dark blue gown and a wide white collar and cuffs. She smiled shyly at him and then dropped her gaze. But William continued to stare, quite taken with her. He decided he must find out from Knox who she was.

The young woman was Katherine Jaqueman, originally from the city of Orleans in France. William wanted to meet her, intrigued to know more about her. So Knox arranged to have them meet at his home.

'Mademoiselle, I'm very pleased to meet you.' William greeted Katherine as they stood in Knox's sitting room.

'Monsieur,' Katherine replied in accented English. 'Have you been long in Geneva?'

They sat down and William spent the afternoon telling her all the places in Europe he had lived and ended by telling her his dream of translating the Bible. He was surprised when Knox's housekeeper announced that supper was ready. Katherine had sat and listened with interest, asking questions and making comments. Knox was busy reading a book, knowing he wasn't needed in the conversation.

For the next several months when William wasn't studying and translating, he visited Katherine at her father's house. Even though she was just twenty-one and he was thirty-two, he knew this was the woman he wanted to marry. And he was overjoyed when she said yes and her father gave his permission. They were married in Notre-Dame-la-Neuve by Knox that November.

William continued to labour over his translation. The work came easily for him, but he was concerned to be careful, checking

Tyndale's translation as well as others against his own. And he consulted often with Calvin, asking his opinion on some of the words or phrases.

'I want this translation to "sound" right, to read the way people really talk,' William explained as he sat in Calvin's study. 'Many of Tyndale's phrases are wonderful, but every now and then I think I have chosen something just a little clearer. Is that arrogant of me?'

'Not at all,' Calvin assured him. 'Languages change. Some words are used for a while and then become less important. That's why we need new translations.'

William nodded and then asked, 'Have you thought any more about writing a preface for this edition? I think the readers would find it helpful.'

'Yes, I've begun to write it. I want to call it 'Christ is the End of the Law.' I should be able to complete it by the end of the week. And by the way, I like your new idea of dividing the chapters in each book of the Bible into verses.'

William smiled. 'I'm trying to make God's Word as easy to use as possible. And I'm also putting in some commentary notes on each page, so that people can understand some of the more difficult meanings, especially in Paul's epistles.'

'My friend,' Calvin said. 'I think you are serving God and his church well with this new translation.'

Two years after he had arrived in Geneva, William collected the first copy of his translation of the New Testament from the printer. He hurried home to show Katherine. Taking the large leather bound book in her hands, she opened it, turning the stiff paper carefully.

'You did all of this?' she asked in wonder.

'Not by myself,' he assured her. 'I had a great deal of help from Calvin and others. And of course, God gave me the gift of languages to begin with.'

Katherine stopped turning pages and read the first verse of John's Gospel. 'In the beginning was that Word, and that Word was with God, and that Word was God.' She looked up at her husband proudly. 'This is wonderful. And,' she added with a smile, 'we'll be able to read it to our baby when he is born.'

William gently touched his wife's rounded belly. 'We will teach him about God and read his Word to him every day.'

The New Testament was well received and sold many copies throughout Europe. So William decided to continue with translating the Old Testament, so that a complete Bible could be published with chapters and verses as well as commentary notes. He worked diligently for another three years, in the midst of caring for his growing family and the English-speaking congregation. He and three other men had been elected as elders the year after they arrived in Geneva.

One day John Knox and Christopher Goodman came to William's house.

'Have you heard the news?' Christopher asked even before he stepped through the doorway.

'What news?' William asked as he held open the door to his friends.

Both men rushed inside, eager to share what they knew. Overhead, William's new baby daughter was crying, while his year-old son was banging on the wall. Katherine appeared from the kitchen with apologies and headed upstairs to attend to the noisy children.

'Queen Mary is dead!' Christopher announced as they stood in the sitting room. 'Her sister Elizabeth[4] is now queen. At last it's safe to go home, for Elizabeth is a Protestant.'

Knox nodded. 'I'll be leaving shortly. It will be good to be home again.'

---

[4] Elizabeth I was the second daughter of Henry VIII.

'You and your family will be coming too, won't you?' Christopher asked.

William shook his head. 'I still need to finish the Old Testament translation. It will take at least another year. But I'm very glad to hear that England has been rescued from that popish queen, Mary. She has much to answer for at the throne of God because she had so many Protestants killed.'

Knox and Goodman nodded in agreement as they all thought of friends who had died for the cause over the last five years. Then Knox cleared his throat and said, 'If you are remaining here, would you be willing to serve as pastor to the congregation?'

'But I'm only ordained as an elder,' William protested. 'Surely you should approach someone more qualified.'

Knox shook his head. 'Both Calvin and I feel that you are the man for the job. You have the gifts to preach and teach. Besides, you know the congregation so well and they know you. It is a good match.'

'I think you should do it,' came Katherine's voice from the doorway. She stood with a tiny infant in one arm and a restless toddler in the other. 'Look at how much you have learned from the Bible by translating it. You should teach us what God has taught you.'

William was silent for a moment and then he said, 'I'll discuss this with Monsieur Calvin and then we'll see.'

Calvin persuaded William to become the English-speaking congregation's new pastor, a position he held for two years while he continued to work on translating the Old Testament. In 1560 William published his translation that became known as the Geneva Bible.

What is the Book of Common Prayer?

If you went to a Church of England (Anglican or Episcopalian) worship service this Sunday you would probably see three books in the pew: a Bible, a hymn book and a prayer book. The prayer book contains what it sounds like, written prayers for use on many different occasions: praise, thanksgiving, confession of sin, etc. These prayers are part of a liturgy, which is a set way to conduct a worship service.

Unless you are used to using a prayer book it might seem odd to have your prayers written out for you. Why would you need to do that instead of using your own words to speak to God? Using prayer books in the church is not a new invention. They have been used for centuries to teach people how to pray properly; not so much about which were the proper words to use, but to show people how God has instructed his people to worship him. Any old words will not do when addressing our great creator and saviour of our souls. Prayer books are one way of showing how to come into the throne room of the King of the universe.

The Book of Common Prayer was first written and compiled during the time of King Edward VI (Henry VIII's son). The Church of England had broken away from the Roman Catholic Church and the church leaders wanted to teach both priests and people about what had now changed in the worship services. The prayer book also provided a way for all congregations to be worshipping in the same way, rather than inventing their own forms of worship, which some began to do.

At the time of the Reformation the main argument against using the prayer book came from the Puritans. They argued that prayer books shouldn't be used because people ought to be praying their own prayers. If they used written prayers then they are only reading them out at the correct time, not really praying. Both points of view had merit, and caused a lot of controversy and disagreement.

How a Scottish King became an English King
A.D. *1560-1604*

William Whittingham returned to England with his family in 1560, the year his translation was published. The following year he was chosen to be chaplain to the Earl of Warwick, who commanded Queen Elizabeth's army. When war with France broke out in 1562, the Earl took William with him to minister to the English garrison at Le Havre de Grace. William distinguished himself by preaching in his own set of armour, ready to assist the soldiers whenever the garrison was attacked. In appreciation for his bravery, the Earl of Warwick recommended William to the Queen for the job of Dean of Durham, a position William held until his death in 1579.

Elizabeth I reigned as Queen of England for forty-five years. During that time she supported the Protestant cause and the churches flourished. The Bible was widely available to all who wanted to read it in several 'modern' translations[1]. The most widely used Bibles were the Geneva Bible and the Bishop's Bible. The reformers, or Puritans as they came to be called in England, used the Geneva Bible, mainly

---

[1] 'Modern' translations here means Bibles that were written in the everyday speech of the people who lived in Elizabethan times..

because of the Reformed notes that were included beside the text, the helpful chapter and verse divisions and the cross references. It was similar to the study Bibles we have today. However, the English bishops and the Queen objected to some of the notes because they were critical of monarchs who used their power to oppress people. Queen Elizabeth was concerned that people would cease to respect and obey the Crown. So the Bishop's Bible was commissioned in 1568 and translated by Matthew Parker and several other English bishops as an alternative to the Geneva Bible. Parker relied on the same previous translations as the Geneva Bible, but did not include any notes or cross references. This Bible was to be used in church pulpits, but it was never as popular with people as the Geneva Bible.

Queen Elizabeth never married, and as she grew near the end of her life, her advisors were very concerned about who would be their next monarch. The closest relative Elizabeth had was the son of her cousin, Mary Stuart, who was known as Queen of the Scots. After Mary lost her Scottish throne because of various foolish political and personal choices, her son, James, became King of Scotland.

James grew up in Scotland in a time of political instability. Each of his guardians was killed by their opponents during his childhood. When he was sixteen he was kidnapped and held hostage for eleven months before he was rescued. Not surprisingly, he came to distrust all those around him. However, by the time he was in his mid-twenties, he had established some order to his kingdom. Elizabeth I died when James was thirty-seven and he was offered the throne of England. The offer came not only because James was her closest relative, but also because he had been brought up in the Protestant church. The Privy Councillors were anxious to keep England a Protestant country.

The Protestant church was not a unified church. When the Reformers began to introduce changes in the church not everyone agreed about how it should be done. Some followed Luther, some followed Calvin, some followed Knox, and so on. In England the principal division between the Protestant churches was between the Church of England and the reformers known as Puritans. The Church of England, or Anglican Church, used the Book of Common Prayer in their worship services. The Book of Common Prayer was written in 1549 during the time of Edward VI and included orders of services for different times of the day and year, with printed prayers, Scripture readings and hymns. Puritans objected to the use of the Book of Common Prayer because they thought it was too ceremonial and prevented personal prayer and worship. They preferred a simple worship service with Scripture reading, prayer, psalm singing, a sermon and the sacraments. The two sides were not always kind to one another, and often took their disagreements to government officials or even the Queen. Elizabeth had no time for these quarrels, telling them to get along together and stop making such a fuss. So everyone was waiting to see how the new king, James I, would deal with the divisions in the church.

One person who was particularly interested in what kind of king James would be was a man by the name of Laurence Chaderton. Sixty-seven years before James came to the English throne, Laurence was born into a prosperous Roman Catholic family. He grew up during Elizabeth I's reign. As a child he accepted the teaching of the Catholic Church, but when he went away to study at Christ's College in Cambridge[1], he heard Edward Dering, a Puritan preacher, and was converted to the Reformed faith. In 1564, Laurence was twenty-eight years old and living in Cambridge when a letter arrived for him. Laurence was to discover that letters had a way of changing his life in unexpected ways.

---

[1] See map on page 231.

One of God's Secretaries

A.D. 1564-1611

'Laurence, there's a letter for you,' Richard Bancroft called out.

Laurence set down his pen at the sound of his friend's voice. He could hear Richard taking the stone steps two at a time up to his room at Christ's College, Cambridge.

Richard banged on the wooden door. 'Open up, Laurence. It's from your father.'

Laurence rose slowly from his worn wooden desk by the window. He had been waiting for this letter for several weeks, and now that it had come he suddenly wished it hadn't. He stretched his long muscular body and straightened his academic gown.

At Richard's renewed knocking, Laurence sighed and called out, 'Patience, patience, Richard. I'm coming.'

Laurence lifted the latch and opened the door. Richard almost fell through in his haste to hand over the folded and sealed paper. Laurence took it reluctantly.

'Aren't you going to open it?' Richard asked, still breathing hard from his swift climb.

Laurence turned it over several times and then finally broke the seal. A shilling fell out and rolled around on the floor as he unfolded the single sheet. His stomach began to knot up as he read:

> 'Dear Laurence,
> If you will renounce the new sect which you have
> joined you may expect all the happiness which the
> care of an indulgent father can secure you; otherwise
> I enclose in this letter a shilling to buy a wallet with.
> Go and beg for your living. Farewell!'

Laurence slowly folded the letter back up. 'It's as I feared. He has disinherited me. I've disappointed and angered him by my conversion to the Reformed faith. Because he's Catholic he will have nothing to do with me now.'

Richard shook his head. 'I'm sorry to hear it. How will you live?'

Laurence ran his fingers through his thick blonde hair as he walked back toward his desk, allowing Richard into the small room. 'I'll have to start teaching some of the younger students. And maybe I will qualify for some scholarships. I can't leave my studies, not when I'm so close to receiving my degree.' He bent down to pick up the shilling that had come to rest by his desk. 'I was just reading Psalm 27 last night and God gave me his promise: "My father and my mother have forsaken me, but the LORD will take me in."'

'Well, that's true, but if you weren't so extreme in your views, you just might bring your father round,' Richard said, settling his small frame comfortably on Laurence's narrow bed. 'You overzealous Puritans have rejected what your queen tells you is the true church.'

Laurence shook his head and sat down in the only chair in the room. 'The Church of England is full of the same ceremonies and rituals that I grew up with in the Catholic Church. According to

Calvin, we should worship God simply in spirit and truth, with praise, prayer, Scripture reading, preaching and the sacraments.'

'No, no!' Richard replied, punching the pillow for emphasis. 'God is holy, majestic and beyond our understanding. Would you come into his presence as if you were speaking to the butcher? We don't just stroll into the palace as if the Queen is of no importance. How much more should we approach God with all reverence and awe!'

Richard leaned back against the wall and pretended to bang his head several times, his short dark hair flopping about his face. 'If only I could knock some sense into you,' he lamented.

Laurence gave a small smile and reached over to put a cloth marker in the book he had been reading. This debate between them was not new. Richard strongly believed that the Anglican Church was following the right way to worship God and especially because it had been ordained by their good queen, Elizabeth. But Laurence was more convinced that the simple Puritan approach was right. The church didn't need all the other ceremonies. Neither man would give ground to the other as they enthusiastically debated the issue.

'Someone's already tried to knock sense into you, if I recall correctly, and it didn't work at all well,' Laurence replied.

Richard's serious face broke into a smile. 'Indeed, and what would I have done without my friend to rescue me? How is your hand? Is it fully healed?' he finished on a more serious note.

Laurence held up his left hand that had a newly healed scar from a knife wound running along the palm. 'Yes, it's fine. I'm just glad I was there to pull you out of that fight. Some of our fellow students are too ready to settle ideological differences with weapons. And you, Richard, should be more careful about how and to whom you preach.'

'The truth should be defended in all quarters!' he responded, and then changed the subject. 'So what great work are you expounding this week?' he asked, getting up and wandering over to the desk. 'Something you need my great mind to assist you with?'

Laurence laughed. 'Go apply your great mind to your own studies and leave me to mine. And if you hear of any students who need tutoring, please send them to me. I need to start earning money right away.'

Richard nodded and left the room.

Laurence worked diligently over the next eight years, earning two degrees and admittance as a fellow of the college. The stipend from the fellowship plus the money he earned tutoring helped to keep him in food and clothing. His excellent academic studies in theology, Latin, Greek and logic led to scholarships and honours that would have pleased even his father. But his father wouldn't have been pleased to hear his son preach. Laurence was ordained by the Bishop of Lincoln to pastor St Clement's Church in Cambridge and there he preached with conviction the need for personal salvation and for the proper worship of God.

Laurence tried several times to contact his family in his hometown of Oldham in Lancashire, but his father steadfastly refused to see him unless Laurence would promise to return to the Catholic Church. So Laurence was very surprised when he received a letter from his mother several years later.

He had just finished a game of tennis with another faculty member when the college porter waved his hand from the side lines of the court. Laurence walked to the net to shake hands with his opponent and then headed toward the porter.

'Sorry to disturb you, sir, but this letter was just delivered and I was told it was important,' the older man explained. He handed the letter over and then excused himself.

Laurence thanked him and opened it. The first sentence told him of his father's death several weeks before. Standing on the edge of the court he carefully read the rest. His father had left money

and property for his mother, his brother and all of his sisters. Then to Laurence's surprise his mother wrote that he too was to receive the same allowance from the estate. Laurence felt tears forming in his eyes and the words on the page before him became wavy. How he wished he could have seen his father before he died. He appreciated the money, but how much better to have made up the quarrel.

'Something serious?' his tennis partner asked.

Brushing aside the tears with his sleeve Laurence quickly folded the letter. 'My father died and my mother has written to tell me,' he explained.

'I'm very sorry. Would you like me to take the chapel service for you this evening? I'm sure you don't feel much like preaching.'

Laurence paused and then said, 'Thank you, John. That would help.'

Laurence wrote to his mother and re-established a connection with his family, but he still felt unaccountably lonely. For many years his studies, teaching and preaching had been enough to fill his days and evenings. But now that he was close to forty years of age he wondered about finding a wife. He didn't have too far to look.

'Come down to London with me,' William Whittaker, master of St John's College suggested one evening. They were sitting in William's chambers discussing their college's respective students and sharing a late supper. 'I'm going to visit Nicholas Culverwell tomorrow. Well, really his daughter, Susan,' he finished with a smile.

'If you're courting, you don't want me there,' Laurence shrugged.

'But I do, for two reasons. The good Mr Culverwell has asked to meet you, after hearing of your excellent preaching skills, and,' William paused significantly, 'he has another daughter, Cecily, who is quite unattached.'

Laurence looked up with interest and his friend smiled broadly. 'You will accompany me?' he asked.

Laurence laughed. 'I think I had better, if for nothing else than to keep an eye on you.'

The two men took a coach to London the next day and were welcomed into the Culverwell home with enthusiasm. Nicholas was a wealthy haberdasher and his home was spacious and well furnished. Nicholas himself was simply but richly dressed in dark green padded doublet and short breeches with brown stockings and a white ruff at his neck, a contrast to the two clergymen dressed in long black academic gowns and black velvet hats.

'I'm so glad to meet you, Mr Chaderton. Your reputation for scholarship and preaching is widely known. Some of my friends have journeyed regularly to hear you on a Sabbath.'

Laurence ducked his head modestly and said, 'I'm glad that God has seen fit to use me.'

'Indeed he has and I have something I especially want to speak to you about.' Nicholas replied. 'But after dinner, I think, for here are the ladies.'

Laurence turned and was introduced to Nicholas' wife and three of his daughters. He took an instant liking to Cecily and enjoyed conversing with her over the meal. She had a lively mind and was well versed in the Scriptures.

'Why don't you preach full time, Mr Chaderton?' Cecily asked as the fish course was served.

Laurence replied, as the servant placed a portion on his plate, 'I think my first calling is teaching. God has placed me in a unique position at Cambridge to educate the next generation of men for the ministry.'

'Yes,' William added, 'and once they graduate, he recommends them for various churches all over the country.'

Cecily nodded with understanding. 'A bit like playing chess. You place your trained pieces, or rather men, in strategic pulpits to preach the Reformed faith, and thereby gradually influence and change the whole country.'

'Exactly,' Laurence responded, pleased that Cecily had so quickly seen his mission. He was already thinking she was the kind of woman he wanted to marry.

After the meal, Nicholas invited Laurence to join him in a small sitting room warmed by a cheerful fire in a stone fireplace. After they both settled into comfortably upholstered chairs, Nicholas began.

'God has blessed me with much success in my business and great wealth. Since I know all this comes from Him, I want to use my money to further the cause of the Reformed faith. I have established a trust fund to support Reformed preachers who are in financial need and I would like you to have some of that money.'

Surprised by the sudden offer, Laurence stuttered, 'But surely there are other, younger men...'

Nicholas shook his head. 'I don't wish to offend you, but I have heard of how your father disowned you years ago and I do know that your circumstances are, shall we say, reduced. You are carrying on a great work for God and I want to help.'

'Thank you, sir,' Laurence said humbly. 'You are very kind. But to be fair I did receive some money from my father's estate.'

'Not much from what I heard, so we'll call it settled,' Nicholas stood up. 'Now I think I have a daughter lurking about somewhere who has no one to talk to. Would you be so kind as to be of assistance?' he finished with a mischievous smile.

Laurence's face turned a little red as his host left the room chuckling. A few minutes later Cecily entered and the pair began to speak as if they had known one another for years instead of hours.

Laurence and Cecily were married a few months later at the same ceremony as William Whitaker and Cecily's sister, Susan. And both couples decided to share a house in Cambridge together since Laurence's rooms at the college were too small. At first the arrangement worked well, but as both families began to grow, Laurence thought he should look around for a house of their own. Around the same time in 1583, an old friend, Sir Walter Mildmay, came to see him.

'Laurence, I have had an idea and I want you to be part of it,' Walter began, his long narrow face aglow with enthusiasm. 'I would like to start another college here in Cambridge and call it Emmanuel College. It would primarily be a seminary to train godly preachers. And I want you to be the Master.'

Laurence smiled at his friend's enthusiasm, but was uncertain about the idea. 'You have enough money to do this? You've already paid for eight new positions here at Christ's College. And where would you build it?'

'I want to buy the land where the old priory stood before King Henry VIII's time, just down the road a piece. And yes, God has given me much more money that I can ever spend on myself. Queen Elizabeth has been very gracious to me, appointing me Chancellor of the Exchequer and has given me many honours. However, I can't offer you much of a salary since most of the money will go to buildings and land. But I must have you as its Master or I won't build it!'

Laurence shook his head. 'That's not much of an offer,' he said. 'But I am intrigued. Let me think about it.'

After much thought and prayer Laurence decided to accept the position. While the pay was small, he would have a place to live with his family, and he could continue the work of training men for the ministry. It took two years to build the stone buildings including a chapel, the Master's house, refectory and classrooms.

For the next nineteen years Laurence worked diligently to recruit exceptional students for the new college, carry on his duties of preaching and teaching, and his own studies in theology as well. During those years he and Cecily had only one surviving daughter, Elizabeth, who eventually married one of Laurence's students.

By the time Queen Elizabeth I died in 1603 Laurence was sixty-seven years old. He thought most of his life's work was behind him and that, even though his health was good, he might retire in a few years. But God had other plans that began with a letter near the end of that year.

'Laurence, look!' Cecily burst into his study waving a letter. 'It has the royal seal on it. What would the new king be writing to you about?'

Laurence looked up from his book, brushing his now grey hair out of his eyes, 'I have no idea, unless it's something to do with the college?' he said holding out his hand.

As Cecily hovered anxiously at his elbow, Laurence carefully broke the large seal and unfolded the paper. Together they peered at the elegant handwriting of a royal secretary.

'A conference?' Cecily asked.

'Hmmm,' Laurence murmured, re-reading the contents. 'At Hampton Court, to be held in January. It seems our new king wants to sort out the church, which can't be too soon for me. He was brought up a Presbyterian in Scotland, so surely he will do away with all this unnecessary ceremony and fancy garments that bishops wear.'

'And if he doesn't? What will you do?'

'Tell him what I think. Wearing the surplice or kneeling for communion are outward ceremonies, which we shouldn't be forced to perform. What matters is a person's heart and relationship with God. If others want to do them, let them, but don't force me or those I teach in this college to do it if it's against our conscience. These ought to be matters of indifference, not ways of determining if someone is a good Christian or not.'

Cecily's eyes widened with concern. 'Are you sure that is a safe thing to say?'

'No, but I'm getting to be an old man. If I can't speak my mind now, when can I? I will write a reply and tell the King's Privy Council I will attend the conference. And, I suppose I'll see my old friend, Richard Bancroft.' Laurence added with a shake of his head. 'Richard's ambition has paid off, now that he's been appointed Bishop of London.'

That January was bitterly cold. The River Thames froze solid and the rutted roads were hard with frozen mud. By the time Laurence arrived at the red brick palace in Richmond he was thoroughly chilled and shivering. Unfortunately, the palace corridors felt no warmer as he was conducted by a servant to a waiting room. There he met his fellow Puritans, John Reynolds, Thomas Sparkes and John Knewstubs. They greeted each other and then huddled around the blazing fireplace awaiting their summons to the King's Presence Chamber.

Just as Laurence was beginning to gain feeling in his feet and hands once more, the Gentleman of the Royal Household arrived to conduct them to the king. Still rubbing his red chapped hands together, Laurence followed the parade into the Presence Chamber. He tried not to gape, but his head swivelled back and forth taking in the beauty and decoration of the room, from the high white plaster ceiling to the panelled walls with sculpted ostrich feathers painted blue and gold. Around the room lit braziers provided some warmth. Ahead of them stood the Lords of the Privy Council to one side of a large velvet covered chair and bishops on the other side. Both groups were gorgeously dressed in the robes of their offices. Laurence felt properly under-dressed in his simple black gown. Behind the chair was an enormous piece of cloth displaying the royal coat of arms. Laurence and the other Puritans were led to a long wooden bench set in the centre of the room and told to wait. They couldn't sit until the king appeared and gave permission. But the king didn't appear. Instead, the Gentleman of the Royal Household returned a short time later announcing that the four Puritan ministers must withdraw from the Presence Chamber. The king wanted to meet first with the bishops. So back out of the magnificent room they went and into the smaller waiting room.

Laurence felt uneasy as the hours passed. Did the king not want to see them after all? Was he just showing his power by commanding them all to appear and then sending them home again? He and his friends used the time to pray that the king would give them a chance to speak and that the king would make the right decisions about the church. Finally they decided that John Reynolds would be their spokesman when they were called.

The call to appear before the king didn't come until the following Monday. Meanwhile, they had stayed in some of the lesser rooms in the palace. As they followed the Gentleman of the Royal House back into the Presence Chamber that day, Laurence began to feel nervous. This time, instead of looking at the room, he studied the king and the bishops who stood by him.

King James was rather ugly but Laurence had heard he had a sharp mind, so he tried to look past the physical appearance. The king's young son, Prince Henry, sat on a stool near his father's velvet arm chair. Laurence and his friends sank to their knees before the king in respect, and stayed there because the king never told them to rise.

As Laurence looked up he saw Richard Bancroft wearing the robes of Bishop of London. Richard's face had hardened over time, especially since he had so relentlessly tried to remove all Puritan ministers from their pulpits in London. Laurence knew that Richard would be a formidable debater in this conference.

'So,' King James challenged. 'Tell me why you Puritans insist on disturbing the church with your long list of criticisms?'

Laurence looked over at John Reynolds, who cleared his throat and began. 'Your Majesty, we only object to those things that are contrary to God's Word. There is no mention in the Bible about wearing surplices or a ceremony of confirmation. The sign of the cross is used as a magic symbol rather than a sign of reverence. And nowhere in Scripture are we told we must kneel to receive communion. These things should be purged from the church so that our worship will be pure and true.'

At the king's signal, Bancroft went on the attack. 'Look at them, Your Majesty; they break the law even as they kneel before you. They are supposed to wear the surplice and yet they come before Your Majesty dressed as common merchants. If they insist on breaking this law, what more will they do? Dismantle the entire church? Who are they to question what has been established for centuries in the church? They are nothing more than radicals who bring discredit on the name of Christian.'

Laurence looked sadly at his one-time friend. He suddenly realised that Bancroft had come to love his power more than God's truth. Reynolds tried his best to respond, explaining to the king and the bishops what Puritans really meant by the changes they wanted. But the king kept changing the subject, swinging from issue to issue and not allowing Reynolds to complete his thoughts. Suddenly in exasperation, Reynolds said, 'Your Majesty, would you be pleased to allow another translation of the Bible to be made? One that we could all agree on is God's Word and what we should follow? Perhaps then we could agree on other matters too.'

Bancroft replied before the king could open his mouth. 'What! Another translation? Is there no end to this? The Bishop's Bible is good enough for all!'

King James waved his hand at Bancroft to be silent. Then he leaned forward to look each one of them in the eye as he addressed them. 'But the Bishop's Bible isn't used by all, is it?' he challenged Bancroft, who drew back and didn't answer. 'You Puritans insist on using that Geneva Bible in your church, which is full of commentary notes that speak against kings and their power.' Then leaning back in his chair King James said thoughtfully. 'What we need is a Bible translation that everyone *will* use, one without all the commentary notes and one properly translated by the best scholars in our two universities.'

'But, Your Majesty,' Bancroft interrupted. 'They're all Puritans! We'll end up with the same kind of translation as the Geneva Bible.'

James smiled craftily. 'No, we won't, because the bishops will work with the scholars. I want Great Britain to have a unified church with a unified liturgy and Bible. So, I want the translation work to be divided into six sections. Each section, made up of bishops and scholars, will be responsible for translating their assigned books of the Bible. When each group is finished, the manuscripts will be checked by the other groups. Then the bishops will check them again. And finally I will check them. Only then will it be published.' The king sat back satisfied with his decision.

The Puritan scholars and bishops exchanged uncertain looks and then bowed their heads in obedience to the king's command. The Hampton Court Conference had come to an unexpected end.

Later that year another letter arrived for Laurence, which he opened with Cecily peering over his shoulder once more.

'Oh, they want you to work on the new translation! How wonderful.' Cecily exclaimed. 'And you're to be part of the First Cambridge Company.'

Laurence shook his head in disbelief. 'I thought that Richard would think I was too old for this job.' Then he was silent as he read the rest of the long letter.

'My, what a list of rules Bishop Bancroft has sent,' Cecily observed.

'They're not all his. Some are the king's that he mentioned at the conference. The new rules seem to be aimed at us Puritans. We have to submit all our translations to be approved by the bishops.' Laurence re-read the first page. 'The First Cambridge Company is to translate the Old Testament books from Chronicles to the Song of Solomon. How very interesting.'

Cecily laughed. 'I can see the wheels of your mind already turning. It's a huge project. When do you start?'

'As soon as we like. I must write to everyone on the committee and set up a meeting time and place.'

Laurence met with his translation team each weekday at Cambridge, using the manuscript books that were supplied by Bancroft. He recorded his translations on the left-hand side of the page. When he had filled the booklet, he then passed it to one of his team members who translated the passages again on the right-hand side of the page. The booklet was checked by a third member who made notes and corrections to both translations in the margins. Then the director of the team reviewed the translation a fourth time. It was exacting and slow work. Laurence's extensive knowledge of Hebrew and Greek was exactly what was needed and with his lifetime of teaching experience he was able to explain why certain word or phrase choices were made.

The project took over six years and involved fifty translators. All the committees were told to use the Bishop's Bible as their guide, but they could consult other translations such as the Tyndale, Coverdale and Geneva Bibles. They were allowed to keep the chapter and verse divisions as found in the Geneva Bible.

The Bible was approved by King James in 1611 and it became the official Bible of the Church of England. The king declared that no other Bibles were to be used in public worship.

A Committee that Really Worked:

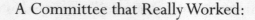

A committee is a group of people working together to achieve a goal. It can work well or go very badly, depending on how willing each member is to do his bit and make allowances for other people's opinions. Committees can be found everywhere, in schools, parliament and even the church. The key to their success is co-operation.

The King James Bible was translated by a committee, six committees to be precise. And they didn't all sit in the same room or even in the same building. There were three locations that housed two committees each: Westminster Abbey in London, Cambridge University in Cambridge and Oxford University in Oxford. Each group was made up of the very best English scholars and church leaders, all known for their superior ability with languages and translation. Each committee was assigned a list of the books of the Bible they were to translate. They couldn't trade places with anyone and they had to work long hours for almost six years to accomplish their task.

The most amazing part was that the fifty translators didn't agree on many things in the church, but they still managed to work together. Over half of them were Puritans, who wanted a simpler way of worshipping God in church services. The rest were clergymen from the Church of England, who thought the ceremonies and a more complicated liturgy showed respect and reverence for God. But each of them put aside their differences when they came together to work on God's Word, and God blessed their translation work.

Once the translation was completed and checked many times by each committee, they all gathered to have it read aloud. King James had insisted that the new translation had to have the right sound to be read aloud in the churches each week. Even as the reading went on, the translators were still checking, making sure there were no mistakes. They produced, with God's help, a beautiful text that has blessed many people for four hundred years.

Trade Winds

A.D. 1611-1760

Although the King James Version was used in English churches when it was first published in 1611, it was not readily accepted by the general public. People continued to prefer to use the Geneva Bible in their homes and only tolerated the KJV when it was read from the pulpits on Sundays. It wasn't until the end of the seventeenth century that the King James Version came into accepted use in both churches and homes.

Laurence Chaderton lived a very long life, dying at the age of 103 in 1640. He saw many changes during his lifetime, one of them in his own family. His daughter, Elizabeth, married Abraham Johnson and they had three sons: Isaac, William and Edward. All three sons emigrated to the New World in 1630,[1] seeking freedom from persecution for their Puritan beliefs. The Chadertons were just one of the many families who said goodbye to their children and grandchildren as the populations of the world began to move in greater numbers once more. Protestants from France, called

---

[1] See maps on pages 232 and 233.

Hugenots, fled from their homes to the Netherlands, England and the New World to escape severe persecution from the Catholic rulers. Wars began in Bohemia and spread to Germany and parts of northern Europe causing people to flee. These wars continued for eighteen years before peace treaties were signed.

But not everyone moved because of religious persecution or fear. Some were just adventurous folk who wanted to explore the New World. Since the late fifteenth century explorers had been discovering and mapping continents and oceans that European eyes had never seen before. Eventually trade routes between these places opened up, allowing merchants and traders to help themselves to the natural resources of each place. North America became known for its beaver pelts and tobacco, and South America for its gold. Diamonds were discovered in Africa and spices and silks in the Far East. And then there were native peoples who could be captured and made to work for fortune seekers or sold as part of the slave trade.

While the work of the explorers wasn't always honourable, God still used these events to open the way for missionaries to follow. Mission work began with the first wave of people into the New World. John Eliot felt a call to preach to the Native American Indians in 1646, after he learned the Massachusetts language. He then set to work translating the Bible into their language and published it seventeen years later. After Eliot's death, others took up the mission to spread the gospel to the various North American Indian tribes.

The Spanish and Portuguese headed mainly for Central and South America taking with them Roman Catholic priests as missionaries. The Dutch sent Protestant missionaries to southern Africa and parts of Asia, settling in places like Sri Lanka, Indonesia, the Malay Peninsula and Taiwan.

In the late eighteenth century, Britain began to send out missionaries too. Missionary Societies were formed to recruit and fund those who were willing to go to places like India and China. One such missionary was William Carey, a shoemaker and Baptist pastor from the small town of Paulerspury. Carey had been involved in setting up one of the first missionary societies in England and was eager to go to India to share God's Word. He, of course, anticipated difficulty and opposition from the local people who might see him as an interfering foreigner, but he was surprised by the opposition from his own countrymen who had settled in India as part of the British East India Company. These men were out to make money. They thought missionaries would just get in the way and upset the good arrangement they had with the local people. The traders and merchants didn't want the Indian people educated or taught to read God's Word. It would make them think they were equal with their British employers.

Expecting Great Things

A.D. 1793-1808

'I hate this place,' Dorothy Carey announced to her husband and sister as they sat in their cabin aboard the *Kron Princess Maria*, a Danish ship. Dorothy was perched uncomfortably on a bunk trying to nurse her fretful baby, Jabez. Her sister, Kitty, sitting in a nearby bunk, was trying to mend a pair of boy's trousers while the ship rolled with the swell of the Indian Ocean. 'And I hate the sea, the terrible food, and the heat. William,' she called out sharply. 'Are you listening?'

William looked up from the book he was studying at the table fastened to the floor in the centre of the cabin. 'Yes, Dolly,' he sighed. 'I heard you, but there's nothing I can do about it. I know the voyage has taken two months longer than the captain had promised, but the storms and uncooperative winds are not his fault.'

'Maybe God is telling us that we shouldn't be going to India,' Kitty said, not looking up from her sewing.

Jabez let out a frustrated cry and Dorothy let out a wail, 'Kitty, please take the baby. I can't cope with him just now.'

Kitty dropped the trousers on the bed and went to scoop the baby up in her arms. 'Come along, my little man,' she told the crying baby, 'Let's go find your brothers on deck and see what mischief they are up to.' And with energetic strides, the young woman left the cabin without looking at her brother-in-law.

William sighed again and rose from his chair. Sitting next to his wife, he put his arm around her shoulder. 'I know how hard this has been for you having to leave your home and to care for our boisterous collection of boys in this strange place. I wish for your sake it was easier, but we are doing the right thing. I know beyond all doubt that God wants me to be in India. Just think of all those people who have never heard the gospel. How can we keep the Good News to ourselves?'

'So why can't Dr Thomas just go on his own? Why do you have to go too?' Dorothy complained quietly. Then she leaned her head on his shoulder. 'I'm sorry, William. It's just I never wanted to leave England. I don't feel God's call the way you do. But I do love you, so I'll try to do better.'

William squeezed Dorothy's shoulder. 'And I'll try to make living in India as easy for you and the boys as I can,' he promised in return. Then he straightened up. 'Now, I must review this Sanskrit document one more time before the evening meal.'

'Oh, you and your languages,' Dorothy moaned good-naturedly. 'One language is enough for most people. Why, when you've already taught yourself six languages, do you need another?'

William kissed her on the forehead and returned to his studies. 'Because, dear wife, the people of India don't speak any of the languages I already know. So I must learn another.'

That night when everyone was tucked up in their bunks, William read the story of the Feeding of the 5,000 from the Gospel of John. When he finished, he patted eight-year-old Felix on the head. 'Just as Jesus supplied what the people needed then, he will supply our needs too. Now let's pray before I extinguish the lamp.'

The following week the *Kron Princess Maria* prepared to dock at Calcutta on the Hooghly River, just inland from the Bay of Bengal.[1] However, William Carey and his family were illegal immigrants and didn't dare risk disembarking at the city. Their fellow missionary, Dr John Thomas, as a doctor could land legally. It was only missionaries who were not welcome in the British parts of India.

'It's a crime to be a missionary under the British law here,' John explained once more when Kitty began to complain about having to sneak in before dawn on a small boat. 'The law is wrong, but the British East India Company merchants are more concerned about making money than preaching the gospel. In fact, they think if the Indian people are converted, they won't obey their British rulers anymore.'

'That's nonsense,' William replied.

'Of course it is, but we still don't want you to end up in prison. Now everyone into the boat. This young sailor will take you ashore and show you where I'll meet you later today.'

Dorothy and Kitty huddled together at the back of the boat, keeping a firm hold on baby Jabez, five-year-old Peter and six-year-old William. Felix sat with his father at the front, eagerly scanning the horizon for wildlife, but in the dark there wasn't much to see. They all scrambled up the riverbank and followed the sailor who led them to the edge of the city where they waited under a huge mango tree for Dr Thomas to find them.

As the city began to stir to life, men in loose shirts and trousers and women in brightly coloured saris began to gather in an open area nearby with fresh fruits and vegetables to sell, along with

[1] See maps on pages 234 and 235.

fabrics, tools and other items. Scents of spices and tea caused the children to look with longing at the food on display. But their mother and aunt refused to let go of them, worried that the boys would be lost forever in the growing crowds. Then they heard a familiar voice.

'Here you are,' Dr Thomas said. 'Sorry I was so long. The customs officials were very curious about all my 'extra' baggage.'

'You mean ours,' Felix replied.

John Thomas winked. 'But that's our secret, isn't it? Come, let's get something to eat and make our plans.'

They knew they couldn't stay in Calcutta. The British soldiers patrolled the streets, checking that all Westerners had the papers that allowed them to live there. So they all decided to head north to a Portuguese settlement called Bandel, where it was legal for a missionary to live and work. But none of the plans seemed to work out. As they arrived in the small city, so did some British soldiers with a warrant for Dr Thomas' arrest. He hadn't paid all the money he owed to various people in England and his creditors had complained to the army. Dr Thomas was forced to return to Calcutta to work as a doctor under British supervision to earn the money he owed. The Carey family were left on their own in a foreign country.

'Now what do we do?' Dorothy demanded. 'Dr Thomas was supposed to make all the arrangements because he had been to India before and knew the country well. We have no place to live and no money to buy food. We don't know the language or have any friends. Why have you brought us here?'

William bowed his head and sent up a silent prayer. 'My dear, I agree this is a terrible setback, but I'm sure God will provide for us.'

But God's help seemed a long time in coming. William and his family had to live in poverty and very soon both Dorothy and Felix became very ill. Kitty nursed them while William spent his time looking about for a good place for his family to live and grow their own food. Finally he heard of a place forty miles away that had a house and land. Once both invalids were able to travel they loaded their belongings into small boats and made the three-day journey to Debhata. But when they arrived they found the house was already occupied. Dorothy and Kitty collapsed in tears from exhaustion and fear and the younger children began to cry too. William began at once to plead with God, asking him to help them. God answered and sent help in the form of Mr Charles Short, an Englishman who worked for the British East India Company. He felt sorry for the Careys and invited them to stay in his house while they sorted out where they would finally settle.

It was a welcome relief. Dorothy and Felix recovered completely, much to William's joy. The children enjoyed playing near the house, although they had been warned of the dangers of lurking tigers and cobras. Kitty was quite taken with Charles and soon they were spending as much time together as they could. Everyone was feeling settled except William. He was frustrated that he had come all this way to preach to the Indian people and here he was living with an Englishman. So when William heard about a job in Mudnabatti, 2,700 miles away on the Tangan River, he decided they should move on.

'The job is managing an indigo factory.' William explained to his wife and sister-in-law. 'It comes with a good salary and a house, and the work is only for three months each year. I can spend the rest of the time being a missionary. And what an opportunity to learn the Bengali and Hindi languages! All the workers can teach me and then I can preach to them in their own language.'

The women exchanged glances and then Kitty spoke. 'I won't be going with you, William. Charles has asked me to marry him and live with him here.'

'So that means I won't have anyone to help me with the children or just be my friend,' Dorothy said bitterly. 'Do we have to go?'

'My dear, we can't live with Charles, and now Kitty, forever. I need to be supporting my own family and doing the work God has called me to. While I understand your fears, we have to trust that God will send us good friends to help us.'

So Dorothy reluctantly packed up their belongings, said goodbye to her sister and followed William and the children to the waiting boat. This journey was three weeks of sailing on various rivers until they reached their destination. When they arrived in Mudnabatti they settled into a mud brick bungalow, cultivated some land to grow their food, and William supervised the indigo factory and preached to his ready-made congregation of factory workers. At last William felt as if he had arrived at the place God had called him to.

William also began another project close to his heart. In the evenings after the indigo factory closed, William began to translate the Bible into Bengali. It was slow work because he was still learning the language himself. He knew there were probably errors, but considered this a first draft, giving him the opportunity for specific language study as well as studying the Bible itself. Within a year he had completed the first two books of both the Old and New Testaments.

Then disaster struck.

One by one, the entire family became ill with fevers. The area around Mudnabatti was swampy and full of disease-carrying insects. Then slowly one by one they recovered, except for five-year-old Peter. His fever lingered, weakening his small body.

William had finally been able to return to work at the factory when Felix came running into his office.

'Father, come quickly, Mother needs you,' Felix said between gasping breaths.

William's heart lurched as he ran after his son along the humid jungle path to their bungalow. Inside he found Peter lying on his bed, unmoving but still drenched in sweat from the high fever. Dorothy was sitting on the side of the bed crying. As soon as William entered the room she threw herself at him. He caught her and held her as she cried harder. Then as her sobs subsided she began to yell at him, 'This is your fault. Peter died all because you brought us to this terrible place.' Then she started to cry all over again, clinging to William.

He held her tight, whispering comforting words and praying silently for God's help. After a short while he helped Dorothy to her own bed where she continued to weep. Then he went in search of some of his factory workers, telling them of Peter's death and asking if they could help with his burial.

'Oh, no! We couldn't. If we touch a dead body we will be outcasts from our families and our village,' the foreman told him. 'We are sorry about your little boy, but we cannot help you.' And he turned away shaking his head.

So William and Felix took some of the chopped wood by the house and built a small coffin. Then they went to the end of the property and began to dig a grave. The hot humid afternoon made it difficult work and they had to stop frequently for cold drinks. By the end of the day, the family gathered to bury Peter. By this time Dorothy had stopped crying, but now she refused to speak to anyone. The boys huddled around their father, not sure what was wrong with their mother. William prayed and then they filled the grave in with dirt.

They all mourned the loss of Peter, but Dorothy felt it the worst. She sat for long periods of time in his room just staring into space. She wouldn't talk or eat. William was very worried about her, especially because she had recently told him she was expecting another child. But she just ignored any attempts to help her. Slowly the family returned to its normal routine, working around Dorothy's retreat from the world. William balanced his factory supervision with schooling Felix and William and working on his Bible translation. A local woman came in to care for baby Jabez and do the housework. After a few weeks, Dorothy regained some interest in her family and began to help out. William tried his best to comfort her when she had spells of crying. Then she gave birth to another boy that they named Jonathan. William hoped that the new baby would be a comfort to Dorothy, but she couldn't cope with the infant on her own. Dorothy was now very ill in her mind.

By 1797 William had finished his Bengali translation of the New Testament. It was all written in longhand and he now needed a printing press and a printer to turn it into a book so that some of his Indian pundits could read it and help him correct the errors. He wrote to the British Missionary Society asking for the money, the printer and some teachers to come and help him set up a school for the local children. If the people were going to have God's Word in their own language, they needed to learn how to read it.

Since there was a war on in Europe,[2] William's letters were delayed and so were the replies. Finally, two years later William received word that not only had the money arrived for the printing press, but eight new missionaries had arrived too, among whom was a printer, William Ward. Carey was overjoyed until he heard that the British East India Company had refused to let them land. They were forced to remain on their ship with little food or comfort.

Then disaster struck in Mudnabatti again.

The monsoon rains were very heavy that year and the Tangan River swelled and overflowed its banks. The water was so high that the entire indigo factory was flooded and William lost all the year's crop of indigo plants and the stocks of dye already made. There

---

[2] The war in Europe was called the Napoleonic Wars. Napoleon, a French general, had set out to conquer Europe involving most of Europe in a series of wars from 1799-1815..

was nothing left. William had no means to support his family and no missionaries to help him with his work. He prayed desperately, asking God what he should do.

Shortly after this, William received a letter from the stranded missionaries with both good and bad news. Sadly, one of the missionaries had died aboard the ship, but the good news was a possible solution to all their problems. The governor of Serampore, a Danish settlement north of Calcutta, had offered to let the missionaries settle there. Colonel Bie promised they could build houses, schools and churches, set up their printing press and he would issue them Danish passports, protecting them from arrest by the British soldiers.

So once more, the Carey family packed up their belongings. Dorothy was still not well in her mind and most of the preparations for the 300 mile journey down the Hooghli River fell to William and his sons, now ranging in age from four to fifteen. When they had finally loaded up the river boats, they waved goodbye to all the Indian people they had come to know in the last five years. William felt sad that not one of them had been converted to Christianity, but he prayed that God would continue to remind them of the sermons William had preached.

After ten days, the boats pulled up to the shore of Serampore, a lush area full of trees and flowering shrubs. There William met with the missionaries who had finally been released from their ship. Over dinner in a house lent to them by the governor, William and the other missionaries discussed what they should do next.

'Mr Ward and I have an idea we would like to suggest to you all,' Joshua Marshman began, nodding for William Ward to take over.

'We think we should build a mission station here and work together. Among us we have teachers, preachers, a printer and a translator. We could begin a school and a church. William, you would have the time to do your language study and I could set up a printing shop to publish your translations.'

William began to smile as he listened, nodding vigorously by the end. 'Yes, yes, that would work very well. And we could all live together, pooling our money to support our families, especially Mrs Grant who is now widowed. I still have lots of translation work to do, which you can help me with, Joshua. And there are more dialects to learn. India is full of so many of them.'

'And,' Joshua added gently, 'Our wives could help care for your wife, Dorothy. We know she is not well. We can all share our burdens as well as our possessions.'

'Thank you,' William replied humbly. 'You are good friends indeed.'

Over the next three years the group of missionaries formed a strong community. They purchased a large house by the river and divided it into apartments to accommodate each family. Colonel Bie encouraged them to build schools to educate the Indian children and to complete the translation of the Bible in Bengali.

William needed no extra push to do the thing he loved, learning languages and translating the Bible. With Joshua Marshman's and William Ward's assistance, the first complete Bengali New Testament was printed in 1801 along with a book about Bengali grammar that William thought would be useful in the schools. Next he began work on the Old Testament, which took much longer. The entire Bible was finally published in five volumes in Bengali by 1809. But these were not William's only concerns. He had also been appointed Professor of Sanskrit and Bengali languages at Williams College in Calcutta when he arrived in Serampore, giving him even more opportunity for language study and teaching. He worked on grammar books for the Sanskri, Punjabi and Telinga languages, as well as a Marathi language dictionary. By 1811 he had also translated the New Testament into the Marathi and Punjabi languages. William loved his translation work as much as he loved learning all the new languages. He was thankful that God had given him such a gift to be able to learn and understand new languages so easily. It helped him as he also dealt with the difficult things in his life.

Dorothy died in 1807 of a fever and William married Charlotte Rumohr the next year. Charlotte was a Danish woman, who came to India to improve her health. She met the Serampore missionaries through the governor, Colonel Bie and became very interested in teaching at the mission schools. She was a great comfort to William when Dorothy died and they quickly fell in love. William was thankful that he now had a wife who was able to help him with the work that God had called him to.

Who were all those missionary translators?

This is a short list of some of the 18th and nineteenth century missionaries and the languages that the Bible was translated into.

William Carey (1761-1834): translated the Bible into more than forty languages in India and Asia.

Adoniram Judson (1788-1850): Burmese New Testament (1823); Old Testament (1840).

Henry Martyn (1781-1812): New Testament into Hindustani, Persian and Arabic (1812).

Robert Moffat (1795-1883): Tswana, a tribal language in southern Africa, Bible (1857).

Robert Morrison (1782-1834): Chinese New Testament (1815); Old Testament (1824).

Henry Nott (1774-1844): Tahitian New Testament (1838).

John Ross (1842-1915): First Korean New Testament (1887).

Samuel Robbins Brown (1810-1880): Japanese New Testament (1880); Japanese Old Testament completed under the supervision of the American Bible Society, the British and Foreign Bible Society and the Scottish Bible Society (1887).

The Bible and the World

William Carey lived the rest of his life in India, dying in 1834 at the age of seventy-four. The Indian people greatly admired Carey for all the translation work he did. Not only did he translate the Bible into the various Indian languages, but he translated some of the ancient Indian literature into modern Indian languages so that they could be read and understood. He also compiled dictionaries and grammar books to aid in educating the people. In spite of all the hardships and disaster that occurred regularly throughout William's life, he didn't quit. He kept working, convinced he must carry out the mission God had given him until the end of his life.

William Carey was considered the father of the missionary movement. He was one of the first to convince churches in eighteenth-century England to support missionaries. And his life inspired many others from Europe and North America to take the gospel to the peoples of the world. As missionaries arrived in each of the countries, they realised their first task was to learn the local languages and then translate the Bible so the people could read it for themselves. But they needed the help from people in their home countries to print and distribute the Bible as they translated it. At the same time people in the countries sending the missionaries also saw a need for distributing Bibles.

In 1804 a young girl named Mary Jones had to walk twenty miles to buy a Bible in the country of Wales because there were none to be found near her home. When a group of Christians heard her story, they formed the British and Foreign Bible Society to make Bibles available first in Wales and then throughout the United Kingdom. But they quickly realised that other countries needed Bibles too. So they decided to support British missionaries as they went to other countries like India and China, printing and distributing Bibles in as many languages as could be translated. Through the nineteenth and twentieth centuries they assisted such missionaries as David Livingstone and Robert Moffat, missionary explorers in Africa, as well as many others.

In 1816 Elias Boudinot started the American Bible Society. As a wealthy American lawyer, he supported missions and missionaries. Through his contacts he began to realise that missionaries needed help with translation and publishing the Bible. The very first Bible the Society published was in 1818 in the Delaware Indian language and in 1823 they sent a gift of $1,000 to William Carey to assist with his translation work. The Society also wanted to distribute English language Bibles throughout the United States. So they began by giving pocket-sized Bibles to sailors in the U.S. navy and later, in the 1860s, to soldiers on both sides of the American Civil War. The American Bible Society was the first group to place Bibles in hotel rooms and produce a Braille Bible for the blind.

These, of course, are only two of the many Bible Societies that have formed since the beginning of the 1800s. In the nineteenth century Iceland, Norway, Australia and New Zealand also formed their own Bible Societies. In the twentieth century even more Societies were formed in Canada, Germany, Brazil, and India to list just a few. Each has been distributing God's Word within their own countries as well as supporting missionary efforts around the world. They also have designed and carried out literacy programmes, because what good is having a Bible, even in your own language, if you can't read it?

Why do all these facts matter? Because God has been using people throughout history to carefully translate his Holy Word and distribute it to every part of the planet. However, there was one more hurdle that the translation process had to deal with. Until the late nineteenth century most of the translation work was done from the original Greek and Hebrew into known languages: languages that already had a well-established history with an alphabet, grammar and lots of literature. But then, as missionaries began to penetrate further and further into remote areas in various continents, they discovered people who had never had a written language.

So where should a translator start? Not only does he have to learn to speak the new language, but then he has to design an alphabet for spelling and a grammar book for understanding. And the only way to do that was to listen and learn from the very people whom they had come to evangelise. As a young American man, Cameron Townsend found it created a whole new set of problems and wonderful solutions.

Cam was born in 1896 in southern California. In 1914 he enrolled in Occidental College, a Presbyterian school, with the intention of becoming a minister. But when the United States joined the First World War in 1917, all young men his age were called up to fight. It appeared that Cam's plans would have to change. That is until one evening when he went to a mission conference, where he was challenged to think about what God wanted him to do with his life.

The Bible is the
Greatest Missionary
1917-1936

'So you don't want to fight, is that it?' the army officer demanded as he glared at Cameron Townsend standing at attention before him. The captain looked the slightly built twenty-one year old up and down. 'Well? Why do you want a discharge? We're at war and your country needs you.'

Cam cleared his throat and began. 'Sir, it's not that I don't want to do my duty. That's why I joined the Reserve Forces when I entered college. But sir, I also have another call to serve...' Cam swallowed, 'to serve God. He's calling me to Guatemala to sell Bibles and share the gospel.'

The captain studied Cam thoughtfully. 'Well, that's probably about as difficult as shipping out to Europe to fight the Germans.'

Cam almost smiled. He remembered what the speaker at last week's mission conference had said to him and the others in the room. She had served on the mission field for many years and challenged them with, 'You're cowards if you go and fight in the war, leaving us women to go to the mission fields of the world. More American men can be soldiers than missionaries. You must answer God's call to preach the gospel to the lost.' And that was what Cam was trying to do now.

The captain's voice called Cam back to the small army office. 'You'll probably do more good in the world by selling Bibles than by fighting. Alright, I'll recommend you get your discharge. Take this paper and see the corporal on your way out.' He filled out a form and handed it to Cam. 'God bless you, my boy.'

Amazed, Cam took the paper. 'Thank you, sir. Thank you.' He saluted and left the office, praising God silently as he went.

Cam and his best friend, Elbert Robinson, whose nickname was Robby, spent the next couple of months preparing for their new careers. They both left their college studies at Occidental College

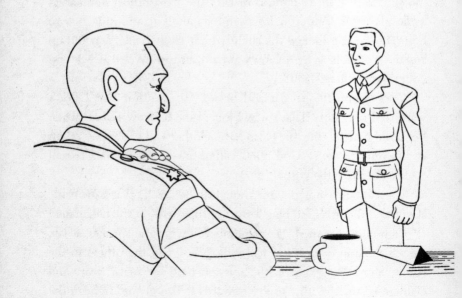

in Los Angeles and took jobs loading ships on the docks. The work helped build them up physically and earn the money they needed for their passage on the ship leaving San Francisco for Guatemala. They also made all their arrangements with the mission board to obtain a large number of Spanish language Bibles. The young men could barely contain their excitement when the day finally came to board the ship and be on their way.

After two weeks Robby and Cam found themselves standing in Guatemala City[1] surrounded by their baggage and boxes of Bibles. Tall, dark-haired Robby and slight, fair-haired Cam rather stood out in the crowd of brightly dressed bronze-skinned people. The street bustled with carriages, wagons and mules all moving about with leisurely purpose. Not far away was an open air market with vendors calling out their wares. In the distance, surrounding the city, were high hills and three volcanoes. It all felt very different from their homes in California.

After getting settled in the home of a missionary, Robby and Cam decided to try out their Spanish on the street. Taking a few Bibles with them, they walked down toward the marketplace. Cam quickly discovered that his Spanish was not nearly good enough. People spoke more quickly than he was used to and they also used many words he had not yet studied. Most were polite or amused, but he didn't get very far with sharing the gospel or selling any Bibles.

'Never mind,' said their missionary host. 'You'll do better with time. Studying a language in a classroom and actually speaking it with native speakers is very different. But you both seem to have an aptitude for languages, so I think you'll be fine in a couple of weeks.'

Cam discovered this to be true. By the end of the first month he was able to converse with more ease. However, neither Cam nor Robby were meant to stay in the city. Many Guatemalan people

---

[1] See maps on pages 236 and 237.

lived in the rural areas and had never seen a Bible. That was where the mission wanted them to go.

Cam set out for Santa Catarina, a small city not far from Guatemala City and Robby went to Tecpan. When Cam arrived he met Francisco, an older Cakchiquel Indian man, who had been converted many years ago. Francisco now travelled from village to village as an evangelist among the tribes in the remote areas of the country.

'Come in, come in,' Francisco welcomed Cam into his home. 'This is my family, my daughter and her husband and all their children.'

Cam greeted them in Spanish, but although they smiled encouragingly he knew they didn't understand him.

Francisco shook his head, explaining in Spanish that his family only spoke their own language, the language of the Cakchiquel people. Then he laughed at Cam's look of despair.

'Do not worry, my friend. You will learn it soon enough. Now join us for our evening meal.'

Cam smilingly accepted a bowl of thick bean stew and a tortilla. Not sure what to do he watched as Francisco used the tortilla to mop up the steaming stew. Trying the same, he popped a small portion into his mouth and was immediately sorry. The peppers in the stew were so strong that his mouth began to burn and tears formed in his eyes. He knew he couldn't spit it out so he swallowed it as quickly as he could, feeling it burn all the way to his stomach. Francisco watched with amusement. 'A little hot for you?' he teased.

Cam just nodded, tears running down his face, and accepted a cup of cold water with gratitude. The children giggled as Cam drank the water in one gulp and held it out for more.

After a few days rest, Cam and Francisco set out on a missionary journey with Cam's Spanish Bibles loaded onto their mule. Together the men walked many miles through jungles, crossing swift rivers and climbing steep mountain trails. Brightly-coloured birds sang noisily and wild animals could be heard moving about in the undergrowth. Everywhere they went they were welcomed into someone's home for the night, and Francisco took every opportunity to present the gospel. But few of the people in the many villages they visited spoke or read Spanish so the Spanish Bibles stayed packed away. By the end of the six-month long journey Cam was more discouraged than when he had started. His Spanish had improved greatly with Francisco's help, but it was of little use to the people he had met. In fact one village man had challenged him with why he only had Spanish Bibles. 'Does God not want to speak to me in my own language?' the man had asked through Francisco's translation. Cam had no answer for the man but he promised himself that he would study the Cakchiquel language until he could speak it well.

'Why don't your people speak Spanish?' Cam asked Francisco. 'Everyone in Guatemala City speaks it. The government uses the language. How do your people know what is going on outside their village?'

Francisco shook his head; his normally smiling face was serious. 'My friend, you must understand a little of our history. We are a conquered people. Our nation once was the great Mayan civilisation. When the Spanish invaded us several centuries ago, they tried to make us all speak their language. But we refused to let go of the customs of our forefathers. So our conquerors ran the country without us, punishing anyone who tried to rebel. Now we live in our remote villages and have no say in our own country.'

'Then I must learn the Cakchiquel language right away. Spanish speakers have the Bible in their own language, but your people don't. Will you teach me?' Cam asked.

'Of course, my friend. I have been praying for many years that God would send someone to us who could give us our own Bibles. I think God has now answered my prayers.'

Over the next year Cam spent most of his time with Francisco and other villagers making notes and listening carefully to the various sounds of the language. Some of the sounds were completely different from English. Sometimes it sounded like people were whistling or clicking their tongues, so when Cam made his notes he had to make up symbols for those sounds. To his surprise he discovered that no one had ever written the Cakchiquel language down. So now, not only did Cam have to learn to speak the language, he had to devise an alphabet and learn the grammar, necessary things for a written language. This was much more challenging than he had thought when he'd left California two years earlier.

During this time he visited Guatemala City and while he was there he met another American missionary, Elvira Malmstrom. She had been working in an outlying village teaching children. When she and Cam met, she was excited to hear about his language project and listened with greater interest than Cam had expected. He found this dark-haired young woman's thoughts and ideas helpful and he enjoyed being in her company. By the time he had to return to Santa Catarina, he knew he wanted to marry Elvira. She readily agreed and they made plans to meet in Guatemala City in July and travel to California for the wedding.

After the wedding, Cam and Elvira returned to Guatemala to spend their honeymoon travelling by mule through the mountains to remote villages, sharing the gospel. By now Cam was proficient enough in Cakchiquel to preach for a short time and be understood. Then they settled in San Antonio, a larger town than Santa Catarina with many more Cakchiquel Indians. A group of about eighty Christian Indians lived in San Antonio and they helped build Cam and Elvira's Guatemalan hut out of mud bricks and corn stalks. Inside, Elvira decorated with brightly-coloured woven rugs on the floor, curtains on the windows and simple wooden furniture built by a local carpenter.

While Cam continued working on the Cakchiquel language and preaching in various villages, Elvira helped set up a small school to teach people how to read and hired an educated Indian man as the headteacher. They also oversaw the construction of an orphanage, a small library and a church building. Within a year the mission at San Antonio was a busy place that needed more workers than just the Townsends.

Both Cam and Elvira needed a break, so they set off to meet Cam's friend, Robby, and his new wife in Panajachel by the beautiful Atitla Lake. They all relaxed for a few days either sitting by the water or swimming in the lake. One day while Cam and Robby were swimming in the lake, Robby suddenly disappeared below the surface. Cam searched desperately for him, eventually finding his friend's body lifeless in the water.

Cam knelt beside the still form of his best friend lying on the beach. 'I don't understand,' he said shaking his head. 'Robby is such a strong swimmer.'

Elvira put her arm around him. 'Something must have happened to his heart or brain,' she said quietly. Then she looked across at Robinson's wife, Genevieve. Letting go of Cam, she went to the grieving woman and held her while she cried.

'Why would God take him away just as the work is getting started?' Cam asked aloud.

No one answered.

Cam sent a telegram to the Central America Mission headquarters in the United States to tell them the awful news. Cam missed his friend and fellow missionary very much, wishing many times through the weeks and months that he could discuss a new idea or plan that popped in his head. But Cam had to admit that God did bring something good out of Robby's death. When the Mission told the supporting churches in America of the loss just as the work was beginning, more people felt called to join the Townsends as missionaries. Over the next two years six more workers arrived, including Cam's brother, Paul, and his wife, Laura.

'Your building skills will be a great help,' Cam said to Paul as he helped him carry his bags to their newly-built hut. 'There's still much to do, and I can't let it interfere with my translation work.'

'How's the work coming?' Paul asked.

'The Gospel of Mark is done. I figured it was the easiest to start with. Margarito is my assistant and together we study a passage verse by verse, or sometimes word by word, looking for just the right words in Cakchiquel.'

'So you have all the grammar and vocabulary you need already?'

Cam shook his head. 'No, I'm still learning as I go. But what a great way to learn and study God's Word at the same time. Margarito is learning a great deal too. We hope the rest of the Gospels won't take as long now. I'd love to have the entire New Testament finished in a couple years.'

Paul laughed. 'You've always had great visions. I'm not sure you'll achieve it in that short a time, but I know you'll finish it. Now let's see this hut that was built for us.'

Elvira was pleased when a nurse, Signe Norrlin, arrived to help in the new clinic. Elvira helped her with the patients at first because Signe had to learn the language. Elvira translated while Signe listened carefully. After a few months Signe was able to understand enough Cakchiquel to ask about simple symptoms.

Meanwhile, even more missionaries arrived in Panajachel. They helped to set up the Robinson Bible Institute (in memory of Robby) which would train Indian Christians to become pastors and evangelists. By 1924, the mission had three stations established to care for people with clinics, schools, orphanages and churches. Cam was kept busy visiting each one and preaching. He continued to struggle on with his translation work, often working late into the night with his new assistant, Trinidad.

Cam was also concerned about the people's opportunity for work to make money to feed their families. He approached some wealthy American Christians and asked them to donate money to build a hydro-electric plant and a coffee curing plant. These enterprises gave work to the local people.

By 1929, eleven years after he began to learn the language, Cam completed his translation of the New Testament into Cakchiquel.

Paul, Laura and Elvira all gathered around Cam as he sat in his small study. On the desk sat the stack of papers of the Cakchiquel translation of the New Testament.

'I almost can't believe it's done,' Cam said. 'I had no idea it would take so long. But we did want to make sure that it was the best translation possible.'

'And,' Elvira pointed out. 'You haven't just been translating. You've been travelling, preaching, and teaching among other things. It's no wonder it took this long.'

Paul clapped Cam on the shoulder. 'So when do we get to see the printed copy?'

'I have to send it to the American Bible Society for printing.'

'Won't they wonder about the new symbols you had to invent for some of the strange sounds?' Laura asked, as she picked up the top sheet and began to read through it.

'I'll send a covering letter with the manuscript explaining what I had to do and why. I'm sure they'll understand it all.'

After a two-year wait, the Cakchiquel New Testaments finally arrived. Cam made arrangements to present a copy to the President of Guatemala, Jorge Ubico. The American Bible Society sent Mr Gregory as their representative with the newly-published Bibles and he and the Townsends and Cam's Cakchiquel translation assistant were all invited to meet the President in Guatemala City.

The president, dressed in his military uniform, greeted them warmly in his expensively furnished office. 'You are most welcome,' he said in precise Spanish. His lighter skin told them that he was a descendant of the Spanish conquest.

'Mr Townsend, I have been very interested to learn about your work with the Indian people. Your schools, work projects and even teaching my people how to plant and grow vegetables can only help them. So I thank you.'

Cam smiled. 'I have come to love the Indian people and will do all I can for them. But I really feel the very best thing I have done is to translate God's Word for them. We have brought the very first copy as a gift for you, so that you may see what we have accomplished.'

The Bible Society secretary cleared his throat and reached into a leather satchel. He drew out a leather bound New Testament with a gold inscription on the front. 'President Ubico, a copy of God's Word,' he said. Then he handed the Bible, not to the president, but to Cam's translation assistant, Trinidad Bac. The young man took the book with reverence, staring at it with wonder. Then remembering what he was supposed to do, he looked up at the imposing president and simply said, 'From your people.'

President Ubico took the New Testament, opened it, and ran his finger along the fine paper. 'Thank you. This work is a real step of progress for our country.'

Cam praised God as they left the government building and then said to his wife, 'Now we have to get the rest of these Bibles to the people it was translated for and we have to teach them how to read them. There's not a moment to lose.' But then he started to cough, something he'd been doing a lot lately.

Mr Gregory shook his head. 'Neither one of you looks very healthy. I'm not sure you should throw yourself into another project until you've had a rest.'

'But we have to take the Bibles to the people,' Cam protested.

Gregory nodded. 'Yes, but I think after that you need to see a doctor. Both of you are too pale and tired-looking.'

Cam and Elvira exchanged glances and nodded. After the Bibles were presented, they would take a rest.

The celebrations over the Bibles were exciting and noisy. Musicians brought out their marimbas, drums and shakers. Everyone put on their best clothes made of brightly-coloured cloth and embroidery. Huge amounts of beans, tortillas, rice and chicken were prepared and the people had a party. God's Word had come to them in their own language.

The doctor declared both Cam and Elvira too ill to remain in Guatemala. Cam had contracted tuberculosis and Elvira's heart had become diseased, so they both returned to the United States for treatment. In the home of Cam's sister, Lula, and her husband outside of Los Angeles Cam's nieces and nephews were excited to see their uncle after reading his many letters. Along with their parents, they cared for Cam and Elvira as they convalesced.

It was a long process. Cam feasted on fresh farm produce and plenty of fresh air. For over a year he gradually gained strength, although the doctor constantly chided him for pushing himself too hard too soon. Elvira's condition did not improve in the same way. Her weak heart prevented her from doing much more than getting out of bed and sitting quietly. Cam was worried that she might not be able to return to the mission field at all.

During this time some friends and fellow missionaries came to visit them. One particular visit by Leonard Legters started Cam thinking about a whole host of new projects. Mr Legters, a minister and a missionary who was interested in Indian languages, had just returned from travelling through Central and South America.

'Cam, I explored all the countries and was amazed at how many Indian groups live on the two continents,' Leonard said, as they sipped lemonade on the front porch, 'and they all spoke their own language. None sounded alike.'

'That means we are nowhere near to giving everyone the Bible in their own tongue. How many do you estimate there are?' Cam wanted to know.

'At least a thousand,'

Cam sat back in his chair in surprise, his glass of lemonade forgotten. He stared off into the distance as he thought.

Elvira's voice called him back. 'Well, we certainly can't translate into all of those languages by ourselves.'

'You're right,' Cam agreed. 'We can't, but I have an idea I need to think and pray about.'

After Leonard Legters left, Cam went for a long walk in the wooded area near the farm. As he walked he prayed, talking over his idea with God and asking for wisdom. It took many such walks and times of prayer before Cam was ready to share his thoughts with Elvira. She was sitting quietly on the porch in a rocking chair when Cam sat down on a bench next to her.

'Elvira, I'd like you listen to my idea from beginning to end before you say anything. Then I want your honest opinion on whether you think it would work.' Cam informed her. Elvira nodded. 'We need to reach all those people who don't have a Bible in their own language. I learned a great deal as I translated the Cakchiquel language, things like how to transcribe an unwritten language and how to work with the native speakers as I translated. What about if I start a school here in the United States for missionaries to learn these things? If we trained as many missionaries as possible, say a thousand,' he said with a smile, 'Then we could reach a thousand tribes with God's Word.'

'Why can't people just take language classes in college?' Elvira asked.

'I'm talking about all the unknown languages that no one teaches. We will have to go to the remote tribes to learn them. What the missionaries will need are the tools for learning those languages. Prof. Sapir at Yale University has started a new discipline called descriptive linguistics. It's about learning how languages work, rather than one specific language. I've exchanged letters with him, telling him what system I used to describe the Cakchiquel language. He says my system is very workable and can be used on more than one language.'

'Does Yale University offer such a course?'

'Not the intensive one I'm proposing. I want missionaries to come for the summer months and study only linguistics and in the end have the tools they need to go anywhere in the world. We'll have the Summer Institute of Linguistics.'

'And the details about where to hold the classes, who will pay for it, and will you be well enough to do it?' Elvira asked with a smile as Cam wound up his explanation with excitement.

'Those are in God's hands. He already knows the answers to them, I'm sure,' Cam replied confidently.

Wycliffe Bible Translators:

Cameron Townsend chose the name Wycliffe after John Wycliffe who translated the Bible into English in the fourteenth century. Cam's plan was for Wycliffe Bible Translators to translate the Bible into all the languages that people spoke around the world.

There are over 6,900 known languages in the world.

As of the end of 2010, over 700 language translations had been complete by Wycliffe Bible Translators.

Over 6,000 Wycliffe translators are serving in over ninety countries in the world, and in every continent except Antarctica.

There are still almost 2,100 languages without even one verse of the Bible in that language.

Nearly seventy-five percent of the world's remaining Bible translation needs are located in three areas of the world: Central Africa and Nigeria, mainland and southeast Asia, and Indonesia and Pacific Islands.

(These facts were all taken from the Wycliffe Bible Translators website: www.wycliffe.org)

www.bible

God did provide the funding for the Summer Institute of Linguistics, and much more. Cameron Townsend recovered completely from his illness and with the help of others founded the Wycliffe Bible Translators. Named after John Wycliffe, the Bible translator from the fourteenth century, the Wycliffe Bible Translators have trained and sent out hundreds of missionaries since 1944 to remote tribes around the world whose language had never been written and who had never heard the gospel. So far they have translated the Bible into over 700 languages and their translation work continues today. They estimate there are still over 2,000 languages without the Bible and Wycliffe Bible Translators plan, with God's help, to translate the Bible into every one of them.

God's Word has now been translated into many, many languages over the centuries. In our own language of English we also have many different translations. As our language has changed over time, so have our translations. Many still like to use the King James Version translated 400 years ago in 1611, because of the beauty of the language. Some prefer more modern translations because the meanings are clearer to them, especially if reading the Bible is new to them. Then there are those to whom scholarship matters most and they prefer a particular translation because of how it was translated. We can also choose more than one way to read or listen to the Bible. There is the book format itself, where you can turn the pages. Or you can download various electronic versions of the Bible onto your computer or an e-reader. There are CDs of the Bible to listen to and DVDs where you can see and hear God's Word read. We are spoiled for choice.

How different from previous centuries! But what is most important is that we, like Christians throughout history, value our Bibles just as they did long ago. We must read God's Word and obey it. The Bible has come to us through the mighty work of the Holy Spirit and the obedience of God's servants through the ages. We have been given a treasure, a precious and valuable book from the Creator of the universe and the One who loves us. It is the most important book in the world. Do you value your Bible? Do you treat it with respect? Do you read it every day to learn how God wants you to live your life? We should be like Job in the Old Testament who wrote about God's Word in this way:

I have treasured the words of his mouth more than my portion of food. [Job: 23:12b]

How to Make a Book in the Twenty-first Century or 'Acknowledgements'

Step One: How to Begin

Take: One idea: The story of the Bible; One author: Linda Finlayson. Combine thoroughly until the author produces a proposal which includes an outline of the book, an outline of each chapter and two fully written sample chapters.

Add: One Publisher: Christian Focus Publications and combined with their Children's Book Editor: Catherine Mackenzie. Let simmer on back burner while editor reads proposal and decides whether to offer the author a contract.

Once a contract is offered and signed, remove from back burner to front burner and begin researching and writing.

Step Two: Researching

Combine: One research assistant/or librarian: Prof. Sandy Finlayson, who can find almost any piece of information he is asked for; Two libraries full of useful books: Westminster Theological Seminary and Springfield Township Free Library; Four librarians: Marsha Blake, Grace Mullen, Karla Grafton, Donna Campbell who found material and answered questions; One long list of books and articles (see the list of books the author read on page 222) to read and read and read; Three experts to answer more questions about church history: Rev. Lawrence R. Farley, Dr. James R. Ginther and Rev. Dr. Carl R. Trueman. Learn as much as possible and make thorough notes.

Step Three: Writing

Begin writing, and keep writing, even when you don't feel like it. Writing is a job like any other and most of the time it just requires work, work and more work. But when it all comes together in the end there is a satisfied feeling that makes it all worthwhile.

Step Four: Editing and Polishing

Take: One husband/writer/librarian: Sandy Finlayson; Two writing friends: Donna Farley and Sharon L. Bratcher.

Combine with your manuscript and ask them to read and make corrections/suggestions. Since they are published authors themselves they know what to look for to make sure the stories are interesting and accurate.

Assemble all their comments and suggestions and determine what needs to be changed. The author doesn't always agree with every suggestion but she must decide what to use and what to discard. If there are any errors in the book, they are solely the author's responsibility.

Step Five: Submit Manuscript

Assemble a good copy of your book manuscript and send to the Editor: Catherine Mackenzie.

Await editor's reply, which will include suggestions for any additional material that will be needed, changes to the text or corrections requested. This requires working closely with the Editor's assistant: Irene Roberts.

Make changes, etc., and re-submit book manuscript and wait. At this point it is best that an author have another writing project to get busy with, so the waiting time doesn't seem so long.

Once the editor sends the author the typeset manuscript, the author reviews the book one more time for errors. Send in corrections and wait. Keep working on that other project.

Step Six: Publication

Publisher sends author copies of her new book which she proudly shows to her family, who have been so patient with her. Her family: Sandy Finlayson and son, Ian, have encouraged her, put up with an untidy house, late meals and having to share the computer at inconvenient times. They are the reason she can spend so much time writing and she is very grateful.

Glossary: What All Those Odd Words Mean

Abbot: leader of a monastery.

Alb: a long linen outer tunic with fitted sleeves.

Amanuensis: someone who takes dictation and makes handwritten copies.

Anglican: another name for the Church of England.

Atrium: a large central room, open to the sky.

Bungalow: a one-storied house with a low pitched roof. In the Hindi language it literally means 'house.'

Cadence: a rhythmic sequence or flow of sounds in a language. It is also used as a musical term to mean a chord sequence.

Castellan: The caretaker of a castle.

Chancellor: president of a university.

Chancellor of the Exchequer: the minister of the crown in charge of England's finances.

Chasuble: a long poncho style outer garment that was pulled on over the head.

Churls: freemen who were employed as servants to thanes or as farmers. They also owed military service to the king.

Cincture: a cloth belt.

Confirmation: A ceremony where the bishop prays and lays hands on a baptised person who is professing faith and declaring their intention to live as a committed Christian. The ceremony also implies that the bishop is giving the Holy Spirit to the confirmed person.

Creed: a written statement of beliefs.

Dean: a church office that is next in degree to the bishop. His job is to oversee the cathedral of a particular city and its estates.

Deposed: removed from a position of authority.

Dialect: A regional or social variety of a language distinguished by pronunciation, grammar, or vocabulary.

Font: a set of type all one size and style.

Fyrd: Saxon word for militia.

Gentile: someone who is not Jewish.

Gilt: covered with a thin layer of gold.

Haberdasher: In sixteenth-century England, a haberdashery shop sold simple household items like drinking cups and sewing notions, as well as bigger items like swords and harps.

Heresy: a belief, opinion or doctrine contrary to the teachings of Christianity.

Hostel: an inn or hotel.

Idiom: an expression whose meaning is not predictable from the words within the expression. Example: 'Mary fell out with her mother' does not mean that she literally fell down, but that she had a disagreement.

Indigo is a plant that grows in India. When it is harvested and processed, a dye also called Indigo is produced. The colour is best described as a blue-grey, the colour used to dye blue jeans today.

Liturgy: A prescribed form or set of forms for public worship.

Lyre: a small u-shaped stringed instrument, played by strumming the strings like a guitar.

Marimba: similar to a xylophone only bigger and played by several musicians at the same time.

Martyr: one who is put to death for their faith in God.

The Mass: a worship service in the Roman Catholic Church that began with prayers and praises, then Scripture reading and sometimes a short sermon, and finally the celebration of the Lord's Supper, where it was believed that the elements of bread and wine miraculously became the actual body and blood of Christ.

Master of a college is responsible for running the college and is given a house and a stipend as part of the position.

Monastery: a house for persons who have taken religious vows.

Monk: a man who has taken a vow to serve God away from the occupations of the world.

Monsoon: a periodic wind over the Indian Ocean that brings seasonal heavy rainfalls.

Octavo: is from the Latin language meaning eight.

Pagan: someone who follows religions other than Christianity.

Papal Bull: a letter written by the pope to the people. It received its name from the bulla or seal that the pope fixed to the end of the letter to prove it came from him.

Pope: means 'papa' or 'father' in Latin. It became the title of the Bishop of Rome around the sixth century.

Papyrus: paper made from the papyrus plant by cutting it in strips and pressing it flat; used by ancient Egyptians and Greeks and Romans.

Preface: an introductory essay that comes at the beginning of the book and explains the scope or theme of the book.

Protector to the Council: a title given by Emperor Constantine to his royal representative at the council.

Pundit: in India a learned man or teacher.

Quarto: from the Latin word meaning four.

Recant: to formally withdraw a previously held belief.

Refectory: a dining hall in a college or monastery.

Sanhedrin: a council, like a supreme court, that was made up of priests and judges.

Sanskrit: An ancient Indic language that is the classical literary language of India.

Sari: a dress worn primarily by Hindu women; consists of several yards of light material that is draped around the body.

Scribe: someone employed to make written copies of documents and manuscripts.

Shakers: a percussion instrument.

Shilling: a coin worth one twentieth of a pound or five pence, or approximately five cents in American money.

Small ale: beer with low alcohol content, a common drink throughout Europe during the sixteenth century.

Stipend: a fixed payment, generally small and occurring on a regular basis.

Stola: a long pleated dress worn by women during the time of the Roman Empire.

Surplice: A tunic of white linen or cotton with wide sleeves. It is worn over an academic gown and falls to the mid-calf. The Book of Common Prayer stated that a clergyman must wear a surplice as part of his position.

Synod: a council of churchmen that meets together to discuss church matters.

Synagogue: Jewish place of worship, originally set up in villages too far from Jerusalem for the people to attend on the Sabbath.

Tankard: a large drinking cup with one handle and often a hinged lid.

Thanes: landowners and warriors. They also advised the king in an assembly called a Witan.

Theses: a statement supported by arguments.

Tortilla: a thin unleavened pancake made of cornmeal or wheat flour.

Transcription: something written, especially copied from one medium to another.

Treatise: a book or essay using a systematic argument on an issue.

Tuberculosis: an infectious disease of the lungs with symptoms of coughing, fever, weight loss and chest pain.

Type: individual metal letters of the alphabet used in printing presses.

Tyre is located in Lebanon, on the coast of the Mediterranean Sea.

Vulgate: the common speech of the people.

Wergild: is literally translated as 'war payment.' It came to mean paying a fine, the amount based on the crime.

Witan: an assembly of thanes and bishops called together to advise the king on matters of state.

Bibliography: The Books and DVDs used to Write this Book

Arora Lal, Sunandini. *India*. Milwaukee, WI: Gareth Stevens Pub, 1999.

Brookfield, Karen. *Book*. New York: A.A. Knopf, 1993.

Burke, David G. *Translation That Openeth the Window: Reflections on the History and Legacy of the King James Bible*. Atlanta: Society of Biblical Literature, 2009.

Burn, A. E. *The Council of Nicaea: A Memorial for Its Sixteenth Centenary*. London: Society for Promoting Christian Knowledge, 1925.

Ackroyd, Peter R., Christopher Francis Evans, G. W. H. Lampe, and S. L. Greenslade. *The Cambridge History of the Bible*. Cambridge: University Press, 1963-1970.

Cannon, John Ashton, and Ralph Alan Griffiths. *The Oxford Illustrated History of the British Monarchy*. Oxford: Oxford University Press, 1988.

Chadwick, Henry. *The Early Church*. (The Pelican History of the Church: 1) Hardmondsworth: Mx., Penguin Books, 1968.

Chadwick, Owen. *The Reformation*. (The Pelican History of the Church: 3) Hardmondsworth: Mx., Penguin Books, 1968.

Churchill, Winston S. *A History of the English-Speaking Peoples*, volumes 1-4. London: Cassell and Company, 1956-1958.

Collinson, Patrick, Susan Wabuda, and C. J. Litzenberger. *Belief and Practice in Reformation England: A Tribute to Patrick Collinson from His Students*. Aldershot, Hants, England: Ashgate, 1998.

Cromwell Films. *King Alfred the Great*. Cromwell Films, 1998.

Dillingham, William, and Evelyn S. Shuckburgh. *Laurence Chaderton, D.D. (First Master of Emmanuel)*. Cambridge: Macmillan and Bowes, 1884.

Drewery, Mary. *William Carey: A Biography*. Grand Rapids: Zondervan Pub. House, 1979.

Edwards, Brian H. *God's Outlaw: the story of William Tyndale and the English Bible*. Evangelical Press, 1976.

Ewert, David. *From Ancient Tablets to Modern Translations: A General Introduction to the Bible*. Grand Rapids, Mich: Zondervan, 1983.

Goldman, Lawrence. *Oxford Dictionary of National Biography, 2001-2004*. Oxford: Oxford University Press, 2009.

Ginther, James R. *The Westminster Handbook to Medieval Theology*. Louisville, KY: Westminster John Knox Press, 2009.

Grun, Bernard. *The Timetables of History: a horizontal linage of people and events*. 4th ed. New York: Simon and Schuster, 2005.

Hamilton, John Robertson Campbell, and Alan Sorrell. *Saxon England*. Philadelphia: Dufour Editions, 1968.

Kelly, J. N. D. *Jerome: His Life, Writings, and Controversies*. London: Duckworth, 1975.

Langley, Andrew, Geoff Brightling, and Geoff Dann. *Medieval Life*. New York: Dorling Kindersley, 2000.

Manns, Peter. *Martin Luther: An Illustrated Biography*. New York: Crossroad, 1982.

May, Robin, and Gerald Wood. *Alfred the Great and the Saxons*. New York: Bookwright Press, 1985.

Morrison, Marion. *Guatemala*. New York: Children's Press, 2005.

Moynahan, Brian. *God's Bestseller: William Tyndale, Thomas More, and the Writing of the English Bible-- a Story of Martyrdom and Betrayal*. New York: St. Martin's Press, 2003.

Mozley, J.F. *William Tyndale*. London: Society for the Promoting Christian Knowledge, 1937.

Nicolson, Adam. *God's Secretaries: the making of the King James Bible*. New York: Harper Collins, 2003.

Oleksy, Walter G. *The Philippines*. New York: Children's Press, 2000.

Peterson, Susan Lynn. *Timeline Charts of the Western Church*. Grand Rapids, Mich: Zondervan Publishing House, 1999.

Pease, Paul. *William Carey: The Missionary to India Who Attempted Great Things for God*. Leominster: Day One, 2005.

Reid, W. Stanford. *Trumpeter of God: A Biography of John Knox*. New York: Scribner, 1974.

Svelmoe, Bill. "Evangelism Only? Theory verses Practice in the Early Faith Missions," In, *Missionology: An Internatioanl Review,* v. 31, no.2, (April 2003), 194-206.

Shetler, Joanne, and Patricia A. Purvis. *And the Word Came with Power: How God Met & Changed a People Forever*. Portland, Or: Multnomah, 1992.

Stepanek, Sally. *John Calvin*. New York: Chelsea House, 1987.

Stepanek, Sally. *Martin Luther*. New York: Chelsea House, 1986.

Tew, Tony, A. Kenneth Curtis, and Mike Pritchard. *Candle in the Dark: The Story of William Carey*. Worcester, Pa: Distributed by Vision Video, 2005.

Trevelyan, George Macaulay. *England in the Age of Wycliffe*. London: Longmans, Green, and Co, 1900.

Trueman, Carl R. *Luther's Legacy: Salvation and English Reformers, 1525-1556*. Oxford: Clarendon Press, 1994.

Tucker, Ruth. *From Jerusalem to Irian Jaya: A Biographical History of Christian Missions*. Grand Rapids, Mich: Zondervan, 1983

Wallis, Ethel Emily, and Mary Angela Bennett. *Two Thousand Tongues to Go; The Story of the Wycliffe Bible Translators*. New York: Harper & Bros, 1959.

Wegner, Paul, D. *The Journey from Texts to Translation: the origin and development of the Bible*. Grand Rapids: Baker Book House, 1999.

Whitley, Elizabeth. *Plain Mr. Knox*. Edinburgh: John Knox Press, 1960.

Withrow, Mindy, and Brandon Withrow. *Courage and Conviction: Chronicles of the Reformation Church*. Fearn, Ross-shire: Christian Focus, 2006

Withrow, Mindy, and Brandon Withrow. *Hearts and Hands: Chronicles of the Awakening Church*. Fearn, Ross-shire: Christian Focus, 2007.

Withrow, Mindy and Brandon. *Monks and Mystics: Chronicles of the Medieval Church*. Fearn, Ross-shire: Christian Focus, 2005.

Withrow, Mindy and Brandon. *Peril and Peace: Chronicles of the Ancient Church*. Fearn, Ross-shire: Christian Focus, 2005.

AUTHOR PROFILE

Linda Finlayson is a Canadian living in the USA in the area of Philadelphia. She has enjoyed working with children in schools, churches and children's clubs. Bringing together her love of books, children and history has given her the opportunity to write the adventure stories of real people.

Linda is married and has one son. She has also written the following books:

Wilfred Grenfell: Arctic Adventurer
ISBN: 978-1-85792-929-4

Risktakers series
Danger and Dedication
ISBN: 978-1-84550-587-5

Fearless and Faithful
ISBN: 978-1-84550-588-2

Strength and Devotion
ISBN: 978-1-84550-492-2

Adventure and Faith
ISBN: 978-1-84550-491-5

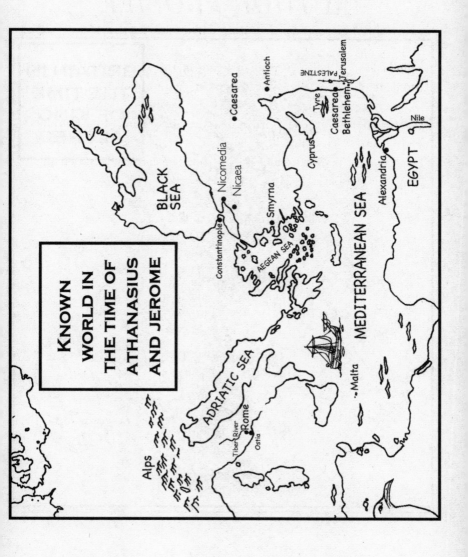

KNOWN
WORLD IN
THE TIME OF
ATHANASIUS
AND JEROME

BLACK SEA

Caesarea

Antioch

PALESTINE

Jerusalem

Tyre

Caesarea

Bethlehem

Nicomedia

Nicaea

Cyprus

Nile

Constantinople

Smyrna

AEGEAN SEA

MEDITERRANEAN SEA

Alexandria

EGYPT

ADRIATIC SEA

Malta

Alps

Tiber River

Rome

Ostia

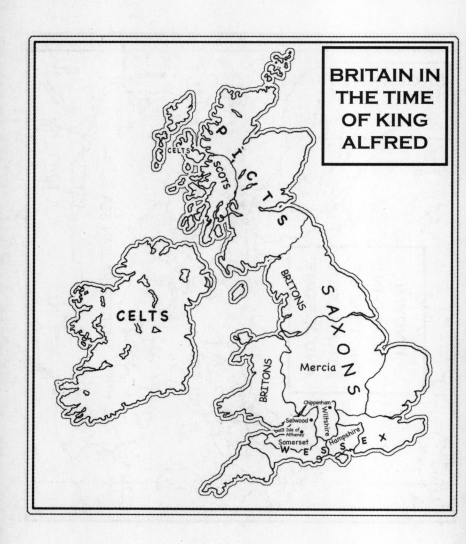

BRITAIN IN
THE TIME
OF KING
ALFRED

CELTS

PICTS

SCOTS

CELTS

BRITONS

SAXONS

BRITONS

Mercia

Chippenham
Selwood
Isle of
Altheney
Somerset
Wiltshire
Hampshire

W E S S E X

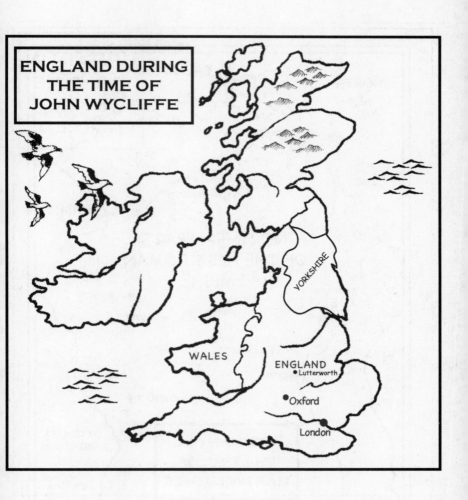

ENGLAND DURING THE TIME OF JOHN WYCLIFFE

YORKSHIRE

WALES

ENGLAND
• Lutterworth

• Oxford

• London

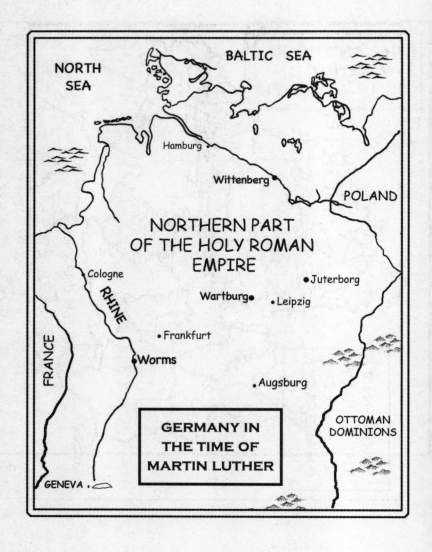

NORTH SEA

BALTIC SEA

Hamburg

Wittenberg

POLAND

NORTHERN PART
OF THE HOLY ROMAN
EMPIRE

Cologne

RHINE

Juterborg

Wartburg

Leipzig

FRANCE

Frankfurt

Worms

Augsburg

**GERMANY IN
THE TIME OF
MARTIN LUTHER**

OTTOMAN
DOMINIONS

GENEVA

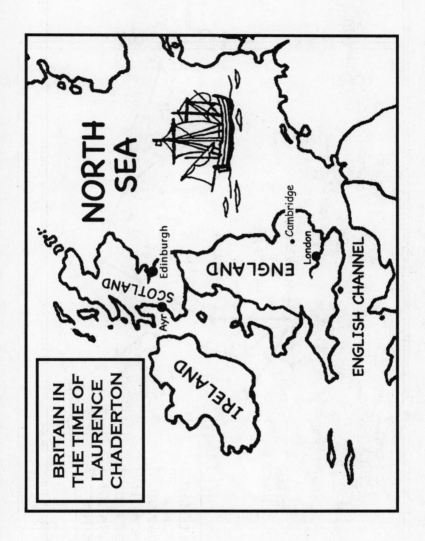

BRITAIN IN
THE TIME OF
LAURENCE CHADERTON

NORTH SEA

SCOTLAND

Edinburgh

Ayr

ENGLAND

Cambridge

London

ENGLISH CHANNEL

IRELAND

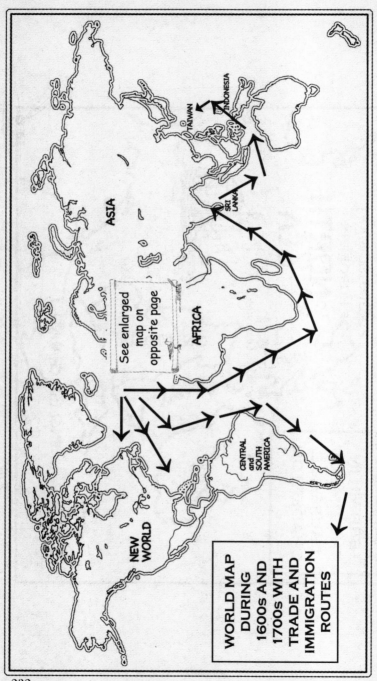

See enlarged map on opposite page

ASIA

AFRICA

TAIWAN

INDONESIA

SRI LANKA

NEW WORLD

CENTRAL and SOUTH AMERICA

WORLD MAP DURING 1600s AND 1700s WITH TRADE AND IMMIGRATION ROUTES

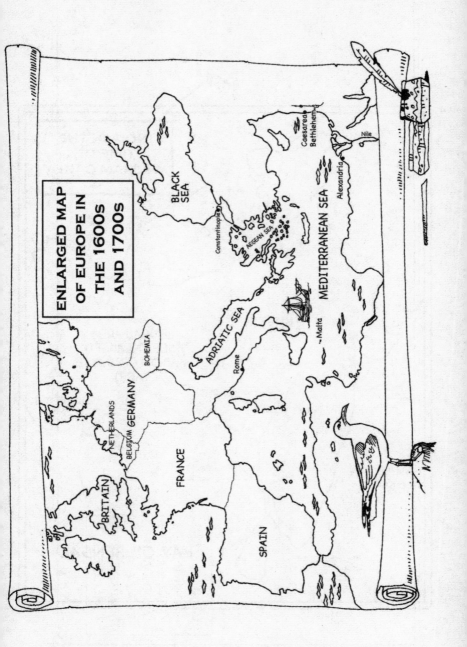

ENLARGED MAP
OF EUROPE IN
THE 1600S
AND 1700S

BRITAIN

NETHERLANDS

BELGIUM

GERMANY

BOHEMIA

FRANCE

SPAIN

BLACK SEA

Constantinople

AEGEAN SEA

ADRIATIC SEA

Rome

Malta

MEDITERRANEAN SEA

Caesarea

Bethlehem

Nile

Alexandria

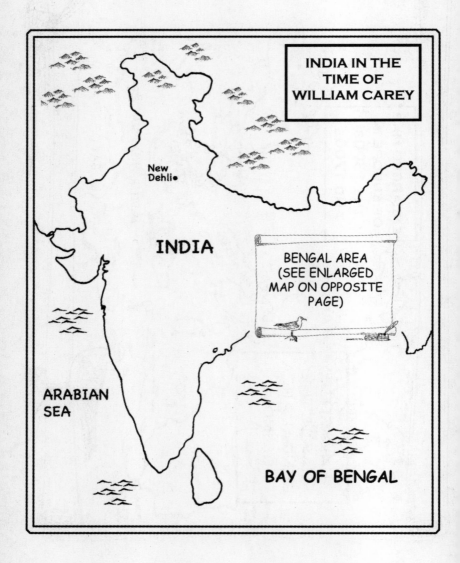

INDIA IN THE
TIME OF
WILLIAM CAREY

New
Dehli●

INDIA

BENGAL AREA
(SEE ENLARGED
MAP ON OPPOSITE
PAGE)

ARABIAN
SEA

BAY OF BENGAL

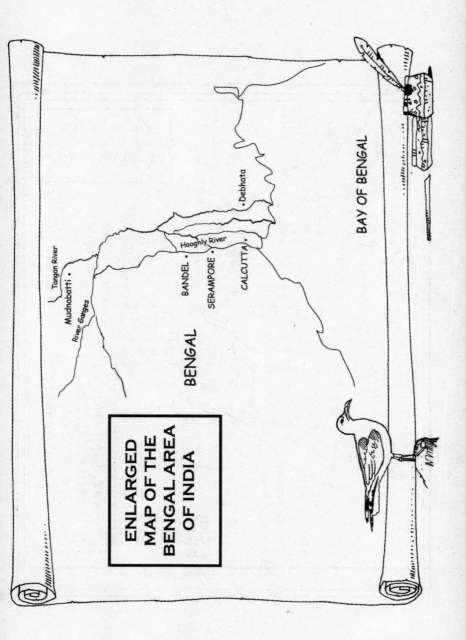

ENLARGED
MAP OF THE
BENGAL AREA
OF INDIA

BENGAL

Tangan River

Mudnabatti •

River Ganges

Hooghly River

BANDEL •

SERAMPORE •

CALCUTTA •

• Debhata

BAY OF BENGAL

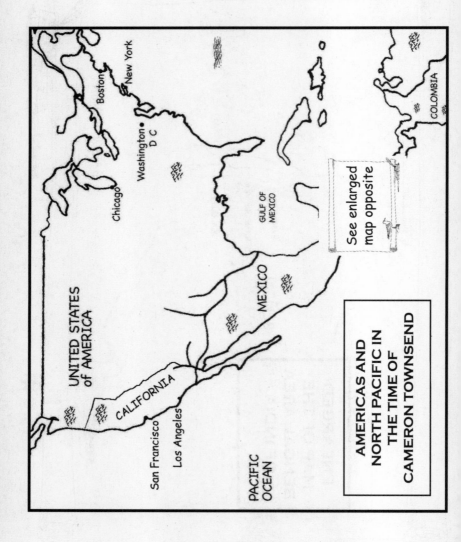

AMERICAS AND
NORTH PACIFIC IN
THE TIME OF
CAMERON TOWNSEND

See enlarged
map opposite

UNITED STATES
of AMERICA

CALIFORNIA

San Francisco
Los Angeles

PACIFIC
OCEAN

MEXICO

GULF OF
MEXICO

Chicago

Washington
D C

Boston

New York

COLOMBIA

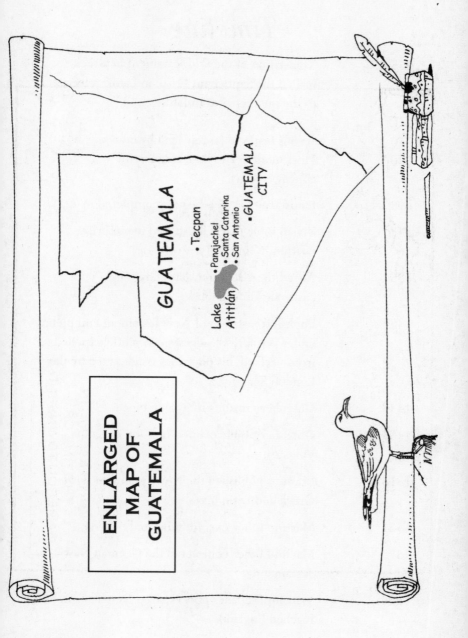

ENLARGED
MAP OF
GUATEMALA

GUATEMALA

•Tecpan

Lake
Atitlán
•Panajachel
•Santa Catarina
•San Antonio
•GUATEMALA
CITY

237

Timeline

255 B.C.	Translation of the Old Testament in Greek (called the Septuagint = 70 in Latin, referring to the number of translators).
A.D.	
360	Scrolls begin to be replaced by books.
500	Most monasteries have manuscript copying rooms.
698	Lindsfarne Gospels begun (completed in 721).
845	Vivian Bible (early illustrated manuscript, written in Tours).
885	Alfred the Great translates Gregory's "cura pastoralis" into English.
1382	English translation of New Testament completed under Wycliffe's leadership; Wycliffe expelled from Oxford, his doctrines condemned by the London Synod.
1434	Gutenberg invents moveable type.
1455	Gutenberg Bible printed (edition of Latin Vulgate).
1516	Erasmus published the New Testament with Greek and Latin text
1521	Martin Luther excommunicated.
1522	Martin Luther completed the German New Testament.
1526	William Tyndale's pocket-sized New Testament reached England.

1530	William Tyndale's Pentateuch translation printed.
1534	Luther completed translation of Bible.
1535	Coverdale Bible published by Miles Coverdale.
1537	Matthew's Bible (published under name of Thomas Matthew, but it was really the Tyndale translation with gaps filled in from Coverdale translation).
1539	Great Bible published and copies were given to every parish church in England.
1549	Book of Common Prayer published.
1560	Geneva Bible published by William Whittingham.
1568	Bishops Bible (revision of Great Bible) published and sanctioned as Bible for Church of England.
1611	King James Bible completed.
1661	John Eliot translated the Bible into the Massachuetts Indian language.
1801	Bengali New Testament completed by William Carey.
1804	British and Foreign Bible Society formed.
1809	William Carey published entire Bible in Bengali (5 volumes).
1816	American Bible Society founded.
1940	Wycliffe Bible Translators founded.
1978	New International Version published.
2001	English Standard Version published.

CHRISTIAN FOCUS PUBLICATIONS

Christian Focus | Christian Heritage | CF4K | Mentor

Christian Focus Publications publishes books for adults and children under its four main imprints: Christian Focus, Christian Heritage, CF4K and Mentor. Our books reflect that God's word is reliable and Jesus is the way to know him, and live for ever with him.

Our children's publication list includes a Sunday school curriculum that covers pre-school to early teens; puzzle and activity books. We also publish personal and family devotional titles, biographies and inspirational stories that children will love.

If you are looking for quality Bible teaching for children then we have an excellent range of Bible story and age specific theological books.

From pre-school to teenage fiction, we have it covered!

Find us at our web page:
www.christianfocus.com

CF4·K
Because you're never
too young to know Jesus